# THE HISTORY
# OF THE RIVER DEE

# The history of the river Dee

by

## Mike Griffiths

# A dedication

I dedicate this book to my wife Jenny who has encouraged me and assisted me from the outset. Together, we tramped the hills, towns and villages, rivers and marshes seeking out supportive evidence for this book. The long hours spent researching in archives and talking to local people was very tiring, very enjoyable and very time consuming.

Without her constant support and encouragement, I could not have completed the task. Thank you Jenny for everything.

© Text: Mike Griffiths/Gwasg Carreg Gwalch

Copyright © by Gwasg Carreg Gwalch 2000.

ISBN: 0-86381-553-7

Cover design: Alan Jones

First published in August 2000 by
Gwasg Carreg Gwalch, 12 Iard yr Orsaf, Llanrwst, Wales LL26 0EH
℡ 01492 642031 🖹 01492 641502
✆ books@carreg-gwalch.co.uk   Internet: www.carreg-gwalch.co.uk

# Contents

| | |
|---|---|
| Acknowledgements | 6 |
| Introduction | 8 |
| Bala | 14 |
| Corwen | 18 |
| Llyn Brenig | 21 |
| Llangollen | 22 |
| Holt | 32 |
| Heronbridge | 35 |
| Chester | 35 |
| Saltney Wharf | 50 |
| Sandycroft Wharf | 51 |
| Queensferry | 52 |
| Shotton Iron Wharf | 52 |
| Connah's Quay | 53 |
| Hawarden | 58 |
| Ewloe Castle | 61 |
| Fflint | 62 |
| Photographs | 65 |
| Fflint (cont'd) | 81 |
| Bagillt | 84 |
| Greenfield | 85 |
| Llanerch-y-Môr | 91 |
| Mostyn Docks | 91 |
| Llanasa | 96 |
| Point-of-Air | 98 |
| Ports of the Wirral | 99 |
| Shotwick | 103 |
| Hilbre Island | 106 |
| Shipbuilding | 109 |
| Tragedies | 114 |
| Crossings of the Dee | 115 |
| Industrial development | 122 |
| Lead Mining | 124 |
| Iron & Steel | 125 |
| Textiles | 126 |
| Piracy & Smuggling | 127 |
| The Last Ferryman | 129 |
| Captain Joe Fellows | 138 |
| Bob Edwards (Master Mariner) | 145 |
| Broughton Airfield | 148 |
| Sealand Airfield | 152 |

| | |
|---|---|
| Lifeboats & Lighthouses | 156 |
| The case of Salmon nets | 164 |
| To the future | 167 |
| **Appendix (I)**<br>Extracts from Mostyn<br>Estate Ports Book | 170 |
| **Appendix (II)**<br>Ships of the Chester River | 177 |
| **Appendix (III)**<br>Other Wharves on the river Dee | 185 |
| **Appendix (IV)**<br>Angling, Wildlife & Conservation<br>Groups on the river Dee. | 188 |

# Acknowledgements

This book came about as a result of a seed of an idea being planted in my brain. The persons who started it all are mentioned in the introduction, but I do not know their names. They do however, have much to answer for.

I am deeply grateful to the County Record Offices at Hawarden, Chester and Rhuthun for their assistance in searching through mountains of material to assist me with this book.

Many who assisted me are sadly no longer with us, people like Bob Manifold and Captain Joe Fellows who went out of their way to help. There was so much more I needed to ask them.

Throughout my travels I met scores of people who gave me information, but whom I do not know. There are also people who assisted my wife Jenny with information. To them our sincere gratitude.

Also to my friend Dan Robinson of Chester Museum. Dan is the official Romanologist and I thank him for the hours he spent assisting me with data and correcting my information on the Roman occupation of Chester, Cheshire and North Wales.

I should like to thank Jim and Pat O'Toole of Mostyn Docks for their help with maps and information, for permission to photograph on their property, and for the historical knowledge they imparted.

I am deeply grateful to my friend Brian Turner and his wife Judith Saxon for their assistance in reading through my manuscript and for correcting it, and for their encouragement to continue when things were not going too well.

Finally, if there is anyone whom I may have missed from the hundreds of people who may recall assisting us, to you also a big thank you.

## The Sands of Dee

Oh Mary, go and call the cattle home,
And call the cattle home,
And call the cattle home
Across the sands of Dee;
The western wind was wild and dank with foam,
And all along went she.

The western tide crept up along the sand,
And o'er and o'er the sand,
And round and round the sand,
As far as eye could see.
The rolling mist came down and hid the land:
And never home came she.

Oh! is it weed, or fish, or floating hair –
A tress of golden hair,
A drowned maidens hair
Above the nets at sea?
Was never a salmon yet that shone so fair
Among the stakes on Dee.

They rowed her in across the rolling foam
The cruel crawling foam,
The cruel hungry foam,
To her grave beside the sea;
But still the boatmen hear her call the cattle home
Across the sands of Dee.

Charles Kingsley

# Introduction

During the summer of 1985 I was photographing on the Dee. My brief was to cover the activities of the small boats in their netting operations. I met two fishermen who agreed that I could accompany them in a boat with a camera, and I eagerly set forth to fish the incoming tide. The boat, which was fitted with an outboard, was to seek flatfish known locally as *flooks* or *flukes*.

The tide on this day was a big one, in excess of twenty-seven feet. It was a cold gusty day making my hands quite raw under the cramped conditions of the small boat. Between taking photographs I was able to help with the netting, which was new to me and very exciting. I knew the area well from my earlier shooting days on the Fflint Marshes, but I had never before been out in a boat.

I was glad that I had put on my old rubber waders and an old mack to keep me warm, and also to keep the salty brine off my clothes. We began to make sweeps with the net catching a few flatfish and then, as the current rose, we were carried up the river towards Connah's Quay. The wind eased a bit and I settled down amid the stinking pile of nets and seaweeds.

Then, on one sweep and with the tide winning the day, the nets were heading for what looked like a pole sticking out of the water. There was something of a panic as the two man crew pulled hard on nets and oars to avoid what they called 'the wreck'.

It seemed that this pole was in fact the main mast of a ship, the *Lord Delame e*, which was taking grain into Rockcliffe Hall in 1948 when she foundered on a sandbank. She was so fast within just two tides that they were unable to move her, and she sank lower and lower in the silt until all that remained of her was this mast above the water. At the time the main channel in the river ran more to the training-wall, so she wasn't a major hazard to ships as everyone knew that she was there.

The crew struggled with the nets and thankfully avoided the mast, while I photographed it. Then, as the current took us back into the main flow, a siren behind us alerted us to the fact that a 3,000 tonne cargo-ship was heading into Summers Wharf to collect rolled steel. The backwash from the huge ship caused the crew considerable anguish because the nets were still out. Shortly after, a smaller cargo ship followed into the Wharf but this time we had sufficient clearance.

The cargo ships under the control of the Dee Pilots blew their sirens and we waved back, although I thought that they were trying to say a little something more, rather than just being pleasant. It was all very exciting and new, even if the wash did come over the side of our boat. We caught fish and I had a story for the magazine.

The tide began to fall back and our little boat touched bottom in several places although it was impossible to see into the dirty sandy water, which had all manner of flotsam on its surface. It was with considerable apprehension that I slid over the side under instructions from the 'captain', and I was surprised to find that the water barely reached the knee of my waders as I walked the thirty or so yards to the shore and the security of the grassy sea-wall.

With the nets safely stored in sacks and the fish in another, the two men walked off across the spartina grasses towards their van in the car park by Flint castle. My skin stung from the salt-air, and my fingers were all wrinkled with salt water and sore because, being they were not used to the labours of net pulling. It had not been an easy time out there, but most enjoyable.

Later that day, just before closing-time, I went into The Old Quay House pub on Connah's Quay dock and asked for the landlord, whom I had been told might help me with information concerning the *Lord Delamere*. In the corner of the pub sat a number of fishermen. Well burnt by sun and wind, their wrinkled faces shielded a lifetime's sweat and labour with nets on the estuary. Broken nails on misshapen fingers, blackened with grime and silt, gripped their stout beer glasses. In hushed voices they conversed about bailiffs and salmon. I imagined this scene a hundred years and more ago, probably in that same corner, with dark blue clad men huddled in talk of bounty and cargoes of illegal alcohol - maybe brandy from a French vessel that had foundered on the lonely estuary.

The men viewed me with suspicion, doubtless my camera bag was the centre of their discussion. They tugged on caps and rolled down rubber waders, and left through the front door for their boats and to examine their nets. The licensee came and we talked. At this time I was only interested in the *Delamere*, so that it could be included in my story for the magazine. The licensee however insisted that I visit Hawarden Record Office, where I would find a wealth of information about the Dee estuary. He also showed me some photographs of old ships in full sail coming in and out of Connah's Quay docks.

Fired by an enthusiasm that I had hardly known before, I made arrangements to visit Hawarden where I received assistance above and beyond the call of duty. From the sepia coloured pages of books, many nearly four hundred years old, I began to research into the estuary and its much under-publicised maritime history. Sadly many people who could have helped me had died before I could talk to them, but some had survived. I was about to enter on an unimaginable journey of discovery, all because of that piece of mast sticking out of the water off Flint.

As a child I spent much time in Northop Hall with my grandmother. To get there I travelled on the footplate of the steam train that brought coal to the village sidings each day at 10.30 a.m., taking empty trucks back to Buckley. Another train came at 3.30 p.m. to take stone, slate, bricks and mortar from the brick-yards, on the line between Buckley and Connah's Quay, to the docks from whence they were taken by sea to foreign parts. The drivers were regulars who soon got to know me and I their cargo. I was too inexperienced to know that I was literally catching the tail-end of hundreds of years of history, and that the few ships plying their trade from the Quay were in fact the end of a very long line of ships that had done the same since Roman times. I was also probably the last civilian to travel that single-line track. When it finally shut in the early 1960's and the last of the cargo ships were sold, I was an adult who did not realise that a vitally important chapter in Welsh history was coming to an end.

The problems that closed the Dee were twofold: firstly, there was the expanding port of Liverpool, which could handle ships several times bigger than those on the Dee, even on a small tide and laden with a cargo vastly bigger than the ships of the Dee. Secondly, there was the trouble that had plagued everyone since the first Roman troop-ship made its careful way from Point-of-Air to Chester along the then winding course of the Dee. Ever shifting banks are caused by the combined effect of sand and gravel being washed downstream on the river, and silt and sand being moved by two tides a day, to be deposited in great banks. This causes the main channel to constantly shift from the Welsh to the English side, and back again. A lack of willpower and under-funding through the centuries saw the little ports from Chester to Mostyn slowly close as the silt beat them and the competition from the railways became too intense. The boats could not compete and one by one they went for scrap or were sold to foreign parts.

Today only Mostyn Docks and British Steel (Summers) Wharf remain, although Mostyn is fighting hard for expansion plans to increase shipping in the Dee. As a conservationist I find my loyalties somewhat divided, but I hope that they get it.

At present, Mostyn Docks can only take ships up to 4,000 tonnes and British Steel can only use their wharf on the monthly *spring* tides. These are so called not because, as is supposed, they only occur in springtime, but rather from their action as they bound forward and cause a bore on the highest tides of each month. They can be quite spectacular in stormy weather, and can come in as much as an hour earlier than the appointed time. This is one of the reasons why the Dee is so feared as an estuary. It is unpredictable and its quicksand is legendary, as poor Mary found out.

One fearsome feature of this estuary is the fact that one moment you might be standing on hard sands, and the next moment on gurgling quicksand that sucks all out of sight. I myself had a close shave below Talacre lighthouse when watching the approaching tide one day. The muddy, sandy silt began to gurgle and I and my dog got away through knee-deep silt that was gurgling around us as we walked, as if in a horror movie, while my wife and children looked on helplessly from firmer ground. It was an experience I shall never forget and it was a lesson I was to learn well. But the quicksand has taken people far more experienced than I ever will be, among them a ship's Captain with many years' experience who was never found.

The only small ships on the estuary now are fishing boats or pleasure boats. The estuary itself is among the richest feeding grounds for wintering birds anywhere in Great Britain, that are fiercely protected by Acts of Parliament. It is ironic that the same silt that killed-off the shipping is vital to the bird population, drawing them in tens of thousands from as far away as Siberia. The whole estuary is now a Site of Special Scientific Interest (S.S.S.I.).

Having left the muddy estuary and travelled upstream, you come to the quieter canalized area known locally as 'the cut'. This is where the river was straightened in 1740 to assist ships to and from the port of Chester. A length of river runs between Sealand Aerodrome on one side and Broughton on the other. These were two vitally important airfields in World War II.

The shipyards that stood so proudly at Sandycroft are now gone. There was a whole range of shipyards from Saltney to Fflint, the Romans having been the first, it is believed, to build ships on the Dee.

Now just the odd jetty appears on the riverbank as you travel towards the old Roman city. There are also concrete pill-boxes that once protected the river from a promised invasion during World War II, and the bases of the big guns and search-lights that hindered the German attacks on Merseyside Docks and protected the ships on the Dee. The big marshalling yard at Saltney can be reached from River Lane. It has become a wilderness since the tracks were ripped up following the closing of Saltney Wharf; only a concrete dock and a pill-box remain – it is nothing more than a playground for children.

All trace of the port at Chester – once the busiest on the Dee – has gone. It is now a property owned by Crosville Motors Ltd, but is still called 'Crane Wharf'. Chester's second port is now a gas-works site. It is hard to imagine that the old walled Roman city was once a major port with a thriving trade and that Watergate Street, the main route from the city to the dock –full of warehouses and contraband – is now a business area giving few hints to its seedy past.

Pleasure boats with comfortable seating and interesting commentary ply from Chester upstream on regular trips. Here they travel the same route used by the Romans who carried pottery from Holt tile-works to Chester for export by sea. But the river here is not deep and with a massive water-abstraction programme in progress, even pleasure boats sometimes get into trouble. The boats now turn at Alford, on the estate of the Duke of Westminster, which is as far as modern boats can safely go.

From there it takes a regular pattern of flow up to Worthenbury where the pace quickens, the first gravel shillets appear, and the Dee loses its canal like appearance.

Above Erbistock it quickens even more and it is upstream from here that the salmon and trout fly-fishers find their paradise. The river here is unnavigable for all but the flattest bottomed of boats, but angling is the priority now, not boats.

It remains in rocky bubbling mode until you reach Llangollen where the Ellesmere canal starts its life from the Horseshoe Falls. Canal and falls were both built by Thomas Telford. Above here the river has altered little for many thousands of years and is classed as S.S.S.I. It remains in the same mode upstream as it runs under Owain Glyndŵr's old fortresses near Corwen and on to Bala where it runs from Llyn Tegid (Bala lake). But the Dee runs through Bala lake having started life as a bubbling spring from the mosses of Y Dduallt, a mountain to the south of Arennig.

I have started my story here with the bubbling spring above Bala and worked my way downstream. I have dealt with all the major towns and villages and the places of historical and archaeological interest along the river, from source to the sea at Prestatyn. But to include everything would have resulted in writing a book half as thick again as a Church Bible. I hope however that I have included everything of major interest.

Whilst most people know the river by the name Dee (in Welsh, afon Dyfrdwy), it is an interesting story of why the sailors and those involved with shipping and the estuary know it as *the Chester river*. In days gone by when ships plied their trade from these ports all over the world, they sometimes became becalmed or needed a line when in trouble, or maybe met another ship. One boat would shout through a megaphone 'Where do you hail from?'

To reply 'from the river Dee' or 'the Welsh Dee' might cause confusion with another river or estuary, or it may be that the call was not clear enough on a rough sea. So the reply became 'the Chester river', everyone knowing of Chester and its then trade with the world. Chester, as an important historical site, caused less confusion and it was generally accepted that the river Dee in its estuarine areas became known as 'the Chester river'. All boats licensed for the river have a CH registration mark painted on the bows followed by a number, CH being a way of denoting Chester river registration. Such letters aid identification for river-pilots and bailiffs.

A quick study of an ordinary O.S. map of good quality will reveal many sites of archaeological interest both in and above the Dee valley. The majority have well-marked access for the public, though some require a good pair of hiking boots and firm leg work.

Travelling from Bala to the sea along the Dee was for me a voyage of discovery. I can only hope that you, like me, will think it a tale well worth telling.

Mike Griffiths
Wrexham
2000

# Bala

The story of 'the Creek of Chester' starts life in the mountains to the west of Bala, where the infant Dee becomes a bubbling ribbon of water after pushing its way through the peat. Here, where it is less than a foot wide under normal flow conditions, it joins two other smaller streams (Afon Twrch and Afon Lliw) before flowing into Llyn Tegid (Bala lake).

Archaeologists believe that the lake formed during the last ice age, some 10,000 years ago, although the valley may have been formed earlier. But the little stream that flows through the lake has always been the Dee, up which salmon, sea-trout and trout have swam to breed over many thousands of years, and still do so.

The lake contains a strange fish called *gwyniad*, which lives in the darkened depths and is known to be a survivor of the ice age, having been trapped in the lake. It was thought to have been extinct until the Liverpool survey showed that small numbers remained in the depths. Anglers from time to time catch some, but the flesh is said to be of poor quality, similar in taste to a whiting. Perhaps it is the pallid, poor quality flesh that has been the reason for its survival.

Legend has it that before Bala lake was formed, there was a small village here watered by the clear Dee. It was said to be a peaceful place until the coming of a new King whose cruelty knew no bounds, and who treated everyone like dirt taking such wealth as there was for himself.

One night the court harpist could hear his harp telling him to leave before disaster struck. Having performed, he went up into the Arennig mountains and fell asleep among the heather and bracken, so warm was the night. The following morning when he awoke, the entire village was underwater and all was lost, including his harp, which he saw floating on the waters but out of reach. The loss of the village and his harp was such that he collapsed and died on the spot. There are those who still say that, on certain nights, he can be seen wandering along the shore-line looking for the harp and bemoaning the loss of the village. Liverpool University went as far as to organise a dive to look for the remains of a village under the water, but with negative results.

Another story of the origin of the lake and the Dee also concerns a small village that was watered by a narrow stream that rose through the peat and moss of the nearby mountains. A heavy wooden board controlled the flow of the stream and a villager was responsible for removing and replacing the board, as was necessary.

One night, heavy with drink, our friend lay asleep in the heather and come the dawn the entire village was flooded, all the homes and livestock

14

having been drowned by the force of water coming from the spring. He discovered that the board had been removed and claimed the area had been visited by the Devil himself. This keeper is also said to patrol the lakeside at night, lamenting his sins of drinking so much ale and allowing the devil to drown his village. With all these people wandering the shores of Bala lake at night, lamenting and moaning, it is a wonder that anyone gets any sleep at all.

There is good evidence that early man did dwell on the ridge above the lake, and especially at the southern end. It has been suggested that some of the earliest settlers in Wales may have occupied this ridge. One story even claims that King Arthur lived on this ridge at some time.

There is ample evidence that Iron Age people lived in the area, and it was on one of these sites at the south-western end of the lake that the Romans built a garrison in 78 AD. They occupied the site until about 130 AD. It was a cavalry camp occupied by the First Cohort of the *Nervi*, which was a regiment from North Gaul. The remains of part of the garrison are still there but, as is often the case, the site was used as a quarry when the nearby farmhouse was constructed and part of the garrison was actually incorporated into an exterior wall surrounding the farmhouse. Conservation is, after all, a largely modern concept.

Excavations on the site in 1855 discovered a stone tablet with carved writing and a statue of Hercules. Both are now on show at the National Museum in Cardiff.

The removal of stones for the construction of the farmhouse make it difficult to tell if the site was occupied after the Romans left around 130 AD. It appears that the Romans had a peaceful time here since there are no signs of major extensions, suggesting that there was no need to expand the military capability. Caer Gai lay on one of the Roman routes from *Segontium* (Caernarfon) to *Deva* (Chester), and also on the route from *Deva* to the Mawddach estuary.

The following centuries are slightly misted, apart from that, in the 5th century, a warlord called Arthur was reputed to have lived in the Bala area (whom some have connected with the eponymous King), and another warlord called Tegid Foel, from whom Llyn Tegid took its name. Following the Norman Conquest, Bala was placed in Powys. A castle was built and part of it (Tomen y Mur) can be seen today.

Llywelyn Fawr (the Great) took Bala in 1202 and set about strengthening the whole area, placing it within the stronghold of Gwynedd. There it remained until Edward I placed it under the jurisdiction of Meirionnydd later in the 13th century.

Sometime in the early 14th century Roger Mortimer became the squire of Bala. He had married Maude de Braose, daughter of William de Braose, the man caught (and executed for being caught) in a compromising position with the wife of Llywelyn Fawr. Roger Mortimer later resided at Chirk Castle (probably the best-preserved castle in Britain). A rather hideous crime that he committed is described under the entry for Holt.

During the wars between the Welsh and English, it was claimed that the state of the banks of the Dee could foretell the outcome of an approaching battle. The eastern bank crumbling pointed towards a Welsh victory, whilst a crumbling of the western bank meant a victory for the English. So seriously was this taken that for a considerable time thereafter the unused bread from a Holy Communion was thrown onto the bank that favoured the Welsh in battle.

Bala was given a Borough Charter in 1324 allowing a market to be held once a week, as well as two fairs a year. Having gained this status, Bala began to grow considerably and soon became famous for its woollen products, especially socks.

King George III himself, suffering terribly from rheumatism in his legs, sent for socks especially made in black wool to help ease the pain. Thomas Pennant, the great 18th century naturalist said that the socks were knitted by the daughter of a Trawsfynydd vicar. Pennant also reported that, on warm summers' evenings, the local people sat outside their homes or on grassy banks knitting woollen goods for export, and singing songs to the accompaniment of a harp. In 1830, no less than 32,000 pairs of stockings, 10,000 pairs of socks and 5,500 pairs of gloves were knitted and sent for sale.

Around this time, Bala wool was said to have peculiar healing remedies, which doubtlessly improved sales. The town itself also had other remedies that included a cure for gout as well as a host of common ailments. Two of the cures for gout were soaking your feet in fresh pig's blood, and trimming your toenails in very hot water.

But if it was the woollen trade that built Bala, it also became famous as a religious centre. Thomas Charles lived in the town from 1783, becoming a leader of Methodism throughout Wales. In 1800, a young girl called Mary Jones walked twenty-five miles bare-footed across the hills of Meirionnydd on learning that Welsh language bibles were available in Bala. On arriving, she sadly discovered that all the bibles had been sold but Thomas Charles was so moved by her act of dedication that he gave her his own. It was this very act that caused Charles to partake in the founding of the British and Foreign Bible Society in 1802. Bala came even more to the forefront of Methodism when, in 1811, Thomas Charles ordained nine ministers into the Calvinistic Methodist body at the town, the first such occurrence in Wales.

Water from the Dee was used to flood the Shropshire Union Canal, built by Thomas Telford in the early 1800's. The then owner of Bala lake, Sir Watkin Williams Wynn who was a Shropshire man, had huge estates and massive sporting rights around Bala, especially in the mountains where some notable grouse-shooting was then to be had. Being worried about the severe flooding that affected Bala from the lake, which was then considerably higher than today, Sir Watkin gave permission for water from the Dee to be used.

Pennant tells us that flooding was a major concern to the people of Bala, and Telford was eventually detailed to look into the problem. However, nothing of importance seems to have been done to solve the problem until the 1950's when plans were made throughout the Dee for flood embankments to be erected, especially downstream in Bangor-on-Dee where £558,000 was spent on the work.

The people of Bala had serious reservations about tampering with sluices at the outlet of the lake and in 1959, during a very hot, dry summer, the level fell by more than four feet. But following the autumn rains this level was reinstated and much more besides when the biggest flood since the major one of 1946/47 hit Bala. The whole of the upper Dee was badly affected, but the sluice scheme forged ahead with the twin aims of preventing flooding and assisting water extraction.

Llyn Tryweryn (Celyn), to the north of Bala, and later Llyn Brenig on the Denbigh Moors, were created so as to supply water to local authorities in England. Tryweryn flooded a village, and an entire community was moved to make room for water. There was considerable opposition to this from people throughout Wales. But even though every Welsh MP voted against the private bill brought before Westminster by Liverpool City Council, the overwhelming English vote secured that a Welsh upland community be sacrificed so that the city could profit by selling water to neighbouring local authorities.

The Dee is the most regulated river in Europe and Brenig is part one of a two-stage plan: the second being to construct a second reservoir near Corwen to draw off the surplus floodwaters from the Dee, and to store them. But this second phase has never come to fruition and it is doubtful if it ever will, as the demands for water from industry are so high. Flood levels last much less today since the run-off is now much faster. This coupled with the anti-flooding measures already taken on the middle and lower reaches, means that the second stage would be a waste of money.

Today, Bala relies heavily on tourism and visitors for its economy. It

17

boasts some excellent eating houses, as it has always done, and there are some very nice public houses here. The butchers still sell locally reared meat, but the woollen mills have gone. People no longer sit to knit on a summers evening, but rather smoke a cigarette and wonder from where the next job will come, whilst watching the sun set or the waves lap Tegid's shores.

Llyn Tegid probably now sees more public activity than it ever did. It is little wonder that the wandering minstrel or the drunken water-keeper patrol their lament after dark, for it would be far too busy by day, as the sailors and wind-surfers use their skills to combat the mountain winds.

Bala is some 160km from the mouth of the Dee, and is the first major town on the journey downstream. It is the centre point for a large surrounding area and for this reason, as much as tourism, is a very busy town. Agriculture is, and always has been, an intrinsic part of the towns' make-up. Agriculture is also largely responsible for the way the land surrounding the river Dee looks, not only around Bala, but also for a long way downstream.

# Corwen

Corwen, about 13km downstream from Bala was a crossing-place on the river Dee for merchants travelling from Anglesey to Shropshire, or from mid Wales to the Wirral and elsewhere. Like many villages and small towns on the Dee, guest-houses, black-smiths and other essential trades set themselves up at such points where travellers met to exchange tales of woe and wealth.

On Caer Drewyn, the large hill that over-looks Corwen from the north, the remains of an Iron Age fort have been discovered. Its position is ideal for, from this lofty position, the Dee valley can be seen from all directions giving an early warning of any danger. There is not much to see today, but access can be gained via a footpath from the A5104 Llandegla to A5 road. It is worth visiting the site for the views alone on a sunny summer's day.

Owain Gwynedd used the site as a base against the forces of Henry II for some time, but little seems to be recorded about Caer Drewyn after this until it became a part of Owain Glyndŵr's line of fortifications across the Dee to Sycharth near Oswestry. Glyndŵr kept men both at Caer Drewyn and across the river at the location known today as Glyndŵr's Mount, which can be seen on the right-hand side of the main A5 roadway as it approaches Corwen from Llangollen.

Corwen developed greatly following Glyndŵr's time, with mule trains serving a large area as well as travelling along what is now the A5 route to and from Ireland. The town also became a centre for cattle drovers moving towards mid Wales or towards England. Blacksmiths were again much in demand, shoeing cattle, pigs and other livestock that were walked towards Dolgellau, which has long been a major market town, or into Cheshire, Shropshire or further afield.

Corwen then became one of the principal stopping places for the Irish stagecoaches, and a thriving livestock market grew up in the town. The market site later became a railway terminal from where animals and other agricultural goods were moved, as well as people. The arrival of the Ruabon to Y Bermo (Barmouth) railway line in the 19th century, surely the most attractive run in Wales, was good for Corwen because it made it easier to export the hardy Welsh cattle, slate and quarried stone to England.

Despite its size, Corwen once boasted not one but two railway stations. The Western served the run from Ruabon to Y Bermo, and the other was a terminal for the (Midland) run from Corwen to Rhuthun and Rhyl. The Western railway served a large creamery just outside Corwen, but this was one of the many subjects of Beeching's axe in the 1960's

The old bridge across the Dee at Corwen was built in the 18th century and today tells the tale of the constant road wear from the increasing size of heavy goods vehicles. Another contributing factor is the sheer volume of traffic that passes through the town.

Near the centre of Corwen is a large pavilion, which is placed behind the new law-courts amid spacious free parking. The National Eisteddfod of Wales was held in Corwen for the first time in 1919 at this site, and it was from here that David Lloyd George once addressed a crowd of over 4,000 people, as did Aneurin Bevan. The original stage came from Liverpool at a cost of £800, but the old pavilion has undergone many changes in its time.

Today there is a bus garage across the road from the courthouse. It was originally a lock-up site where tramps were allowed to stay the night, earning their lodgings from cutting one hundredweight of stone each per day from a local quarry, the stone then being used for road chipping. Such establishments were once common in many towns, and especially in ports. The rooms were fitted with ropes strung systematically across the room; and the better rooms also had a bench to sit upon. The tramp was entitled to sleep by using the rope as support, *in-lieu* of payment. In Liverpool these establishments were known locally as *the tuppeny leans* and gave rise to the saying 'I could sleep on a clothes line'. The old workhouse is preserved as a listed building, and is now open to visitors daily. Having been built in the 1830's, it was then known as The Corwen Union Workhouse.

At the rear of the churchyard is the old Corwen College. A William Eyton left money in 1709 for the building to be established for six widows of former clergymen. A strange provision of his will was that the widows meet the upkeep of the building?

The Parish Church is very pleasant. While lacking any historical events of great note, it does in part date from the 13th century, and has one interesting feature. In the southern doorway, there is a dagger mark in the stonework that clearly shows the outline of the weapon. Folklore has it that Owain Glyndŵr, in a violent fit of temper, threw his dagger so forcefully that it implanted itself into the stonework, and that the mark has been there since the very early 1400's.

Corwen has had, in its time, no less than eleven public houses, a hospital, lock-up, courtrooms, stagecoach post, two railway stations and several other business premises. The most famous pub is the *Owain Glyndŵr* and it was here that George Borrow stayed in Corwen on his journey around Wales. He records in his book *Wild Wales* that he found it 'a most pleasurable place to stop'.

Near Corwen on the A5 stand the old 'Almshouses', and Rug Chapel on the A494 is also well worth a visit to see the wonderful interior. This property is now under the control of CADW, the Welsh Monuments Trust. Colonel William Salusbury (1580-1660) built the chapel of Holy Trinity at Rug in 1637, and he was also the benefactor of the wonderful Gothic styled Almshouses nearby. A staunch Royalist during the English Civil War, he was at one time the governor of Denbigh castle, and a large stone cross within the grounds of Rug estate is said to have come from Denbigh castle, having been moved there for Salusbury. The chapel and the Rug estate is now the property of Lord Newborough, having passed from the Salusbury's to the Wynn family, and through them to the present owner.

A fragment of a tile of the 20th Legion was found where Afon Alwen runs into the river Dee (Afon Dyfrdwy) on the Rug estate. It is thought that there possibly was a small Roman building here, maybe built during the Scapulan campaign of AD 48. There is also speculation that a Roman road ran through the area, linking Corwen with the cavalry camp at Caer Gai. There is further possibility of a road linking across the Clwydian range to the lead mines at Mynydd Halkyn. It is further speculated that a small fort, possibly at Dinorben, was built to protect that route.

The beautiful church at Llangar also lies on land belonging to the

Newboroughs. The church can be reached by travelling through Corwen towards Bala on the A5, and soon turning left on to the B4401 Llandrillo/ Cynwyd road. Llangar Church is seen shortly just below the roadway, with magnificent views of the river Dee. Parking is easy as there is a substantial grass verge there.

Llangar Church is said to date from the late 12th or early 13th century. A story claims that it was once known as Llan Garw Gwyn (the church of the white deer), such an animal having been disturbed from a thicket that grew where the church now stands. Another claims that it was once a site of military fortification connected to nearby Caer Wern, although there is no evidence to support that either this site or Caer Wern were ever of military use. (Caer Wern is opposite Caer Drewyn across the valley of the Dee.) In 1291 Llangar was under the control of the Bishop of St Asaph and valued at £4. It is now, like Rug, under the control of CADW, who can supply further information.

Like many towns in many parts of Wales, Corwen today is at a crossroads in its history. The infrastructure of the agricultural society in the surrounding areas is undergoing pressures that have never before been witnessed by the, mainly Welsh speaking, agricultural community. The social structure of Corwen the town is directly affected by this, as it is by pressures from further afield. Tourism has not been an easy option for towns such as Corwen, in the way it has upstream at Bala or downstream at Llangollen. The very infrastructure of the town is being torn apart, as is the road itself, by the heavy traffic along the A5. A new by-pass is planned which would probably save the buildings of the town and its historic bridge, but what of the people who live here? Llangollen Railway Society, although plagued by problems, is re-laying the old Ruabon to Y Bermo line and is not far from Corwen itself. Maybe tourism will be Corwen's saviour after all.

## Llyn Brenig

Llyn Brenig was opened in 1976 in the valley of Afon Brenig. It cost over £11,960,000 and covers 920 acres, holding 13,500 million gallons of water. Smallholdings were affected by its construction and the remains of some of the *Hafodau* can still be seen above the water line. The *Hafod* was where farmers and their families lived during the summer months, having brought their animals to graze the uplands. The winter months would be spent at the *Hendre*, which was at a lower altitude and usually consisted of superior land. The practise continued from medieval times until the late 18th century, when many of the *Hafodau* became farms in their own right. Hafod Lom, famous for its cultural activities and entertainment during the 17th and 18th centuries, lies under the waters of Llyn Brenig. Work on the construction of the dam however showed that the history of the valley of Afon Brenig went back much further than the times of the Hafod and Hendre system. Archaeological finds included Bronze Age cairns, barrows and other monuments, dating from some time between 2000-1500 BC. Some of the cairns were reconstructed at the top of the valley, and are now part of the heritage trail. There is also an island, one of three, with a Barrow on it in the lake. Apart from the archaeological interest, Llyn Brenig offers fine fishing and boating. A large area of the lake is protected as a nature reserve and in winter, weather permitting, some interesting species arrive here. Also, both red and black grouse are found in the heather of the surrounding moors. Afon Brenig, which forms and drains Llyn Brenig, runs into Afon Alwen at Pentrellyncymer. Afon Alwen, forming and draining Llyn Alwen (to the west), in turn feeds into the river Dee. Brenig is well marked off the A5 at Cerrigydrudion.

# Llangollen

Llangollen gets its name from St Collen, a 7th century saint whom, legend has it, lived in a cave in the Berwyn mountains near Llangollen. Collen was a soldier who fought against Julian the Apostate, a Roman Emperor born in Constantinople who was the nephew of Constantine the Great. Julian became very anti-Christian but was eventually killed in a battle against the Persians. After the fighting was over, Collen apparently gave his life to Christ and sought a simple existence. He lived in the cave along with his wife.

High above (over 1,000 feet) Llangollen lies the imposing ruins of Castell Dinas Brân, which are presently being renovated because of their historical interest. The site is first recorded in the 12th century in connection with Gruffudd ap Madog who reigned over Powys. Many strange stories are connected to the site, the majority of them positively mythical, and the others being shrouded in such mystery as to also appear mythical.

What is certain is that its lofty position made it easily defendable, any invading force being visible from a long way off. The castle also possessed its own fresh water supply. Its construction included a deep moat all round. But, even taking all the advantages that the site held into consideration, it constantly changed between Welsh and Norman hands during the 12th and 13th century. Finally falling into the hands of Edward I, it was handed to the Earl of Surrey as recompense for owed favours. Owain Glyndŵr, however, used Castell Dinas Brân as one of his forts, and seems to have been the last militarily minded occupant. Sometime after 1495 it passed back to the English Crown and is today under the control of CADW.

The ruins of Valle Crucis Abbey can be found to the right of the A542 between Llangollen and the Horseshoe Pass (Bwlch yr Oernant). Founded by Cistercian monks in 1200, the benefactor was Madog ap Gruffudd, the Prince of Powys and son of Gruffudd ap Madog who was mentioned in connection with Castell Dinas Brân. The Cistercians, seeking a life of peace and quiet and self-sufficiency, found that Valle Crucis was ideally suited. The Dee flowed half a mile away, offering abundant supplies of trout, salmon and sea trout. They also built carp pools within the Abbey grounds which can still be seen today, still containing fish though not related to the original occupants.

The Abbey, known in Welsh as Abaty Glyn-y-Groes, became one of the centres of Welsh religious life. Iolo Goch, one of the greatest of the poets of his day, is buried there. Late in the 13th century it was destroyed by fire, but lovingly rebuilt. Henry VIII's campaign against the monasteries saw it destroyed again, this time never to be rebuilt. The Abbots' house has however been rebuilt, and is open to visitors in summertime. The sheer tranquillity of the ruins is somewhat marred by the nearby caravan/ camping site, but it is still a very beautiful and peaceful place and well worth a visit.

In a field a little further along the A542 towards the pass, and also on the right hand side of the road, a large stone can be seen. This is Eliseg's Pillar, thought to have been erected for Eliseg, Prince of Powys, in 607 AD following the battle of Chester. It is claimed to be the oldest inscribed pillar anywhere in Britain although much of the inscription has by now eroded. When erected it is estimated to have been in excess of twelve feet in height, possibly with a Celtic cross on top. Thomas Pennant estimated it at twelve feet when he sketched it in 1770; whether this was an exaggeration, whether the stone has since been used as a source for smaller stones, or whether Pennant had small feet is unclear, but today it stands at just over six feet tall. Pennant described it as being the finest inscribed pillar of the post-Roman era. In 1779 the pillar toppled over and when it was re-erected, the area around it was carefully examined as it was thought to have been the site of the grave of Eliseg himself. The remains of a very tall man were actually found there, but whether this was Eliseg or not will probably be a perpetual mystery.

About three miles towards the pass from Valle Crucis, down a narrow lane that leads to the hamlet of Eglwyseg and again to the right of the A542, is Plas yn Eglwyseg. Built in 1563, this is a beautifully restored

Elizabethan Manor House that has retained its black and white livery. It was here that Oliver Cromwell's brother-in-law, Colonel John Jones, lived. He was one of the signatories on the warrant for the death of Charles I. Before the present house was built, the site is said to have housed the home and court of Cadwgan, Prince of Powys. The house has also, in its time, been the hunting lodge for the Wynnstay Estate, which has the shooting on the mountains all around. The property, now in private hands, has been beautifully restored.

The Ellesmere Canal Company was seen as the saviour of the numerous mining and quarrying companies in the hills around Llangollen. The idea also probably appealed, at first, to the mill owners of the area. Pack mules had been all well and good, but transporting cumbersome slates and other produce by such slow and unwieldy means did nothing for profit margins. The Canal Company's scheme offered a means of transporting far more produce than ever before to more or less any part of England, and little bits of Wales. The ambitious plan involved linking the Dee with the river Severn through a canal system that in its turn was linked to a national (read such as England) network. Cities such as Chester that had greatly depended on the sea as its main source of wealth would thereafter be connected to previously landlocked markets all over the country. The Dee's part in the great scheme of things was as the provider of water, which could itself be transported to where it was needed by the same canal system.

Thomas Telford was given the task of bringing the ambitious scheme to fruition. The construction of the canal, however, was by no means simple, and has in itself been the subject of several books. One of the biggest problems was the Dee valley itself, which Telford solved with one his greatest feats of engineering. His famous aqueduct at Pontcysyllte has, since its construction, been a major tourist attraction in itself. Opened before a crowd of over 10,000 and a brass band in 1805, its arches soar over 100 feet above the river. That the building cost over £47,000 gives some indication of the size of this project alone.

One of the canals' biggest problems, however, was partly caused by the falls that Telford built to the west of Llangollen. The 'Horseshoe Falls', so called because of their shape, was actually built so as to divert water from the Dee into the mouth of the new canal system, this method of extraction being still in use today. It was completed by 1805 with sluices here and at Llyn Tegid (Bala lake) so as to control the flow of the water. The volume of water needed to flood the canal, however, caused enormous problems for the inhabitants who depended on the 'old' river Dee for their living.

Many mills were set on the banks of the river, upstream and downstream of Llangollen. Their water-wheels were set so as to utilise the power of the water. However, when the sluices were opened and the water was diverted, the level of the river dropped substantially. Mills situated downstream of the falls at Pentrefelin, Mile-end and Llangollen town centre all suffered severely, and began proceedings against the Canal Company.

Liability was admitted in 1811, thus saving an expensive court case, with £312 being paid in compensation. The following year Pentrefelin again claimed for loss of trade, and again compensation was awarded. In addition, the Rhiwlas Estate was awarded £250 for flooding near Bala, due to the increased water level in the upper Dee that was attributed to the false falls (Horseshoe) at Llantysilio. An Act of Parliament of 1830 allowed the Canal Company to purchase Dee Mills at Chester, on the Old Dee Bridge. Having done so, they sub-let it, but the new tenants soon sued for loss of earnings due to extraction of water at Llantysilio, for the canal. An enquiry upheld the complaint. Claims were made again and again, and hardly ever disputed, that the Canal Company was taking too much water from the river and, in doing so, affecting people and businesses all the way from Bala to Chester. Regular payments for loss of earnings were agreed out of court until, in 1880, the Canal Company conceded to pay £300 annually to the mills by way of compensation, only to turn-turtle and withdraw the agreement. The resulting litigation brought an end to the battles between the mill-owners and the Canal Company with a twenty-one year agreement on compensation.

The canal also faced other problems, especially near where Llangollen golf club is today. The angles of the corners in a dogleg section were very acute, as the land-strip was too narrow. Telford had warned of potential trouble on certain sections but, as ever, money talked and the canal was built. The worst accident caused by the canal was to occur, however, on this very section. At 4.33am on the morning of Friday, September 7, 1945, a mail and milk train left Ruabon for Y Bermo (Barmouth), intending to call at Llangollen railway station. Fifteen minutes out of Ruabon, she was at full-steam and travelling fast when she hit a substantial amount of water that had come from the canal and damaged the track near the Sun Bank Inn at Trefor. The train was washed away down a steep bank, killing the driver. The same spot caused severe trouble in the 1970s when the canal almost drained away over-night. It took some twelve months for the damage to be repaired.

The canal, however, proved to be profitable for a time, carrying stone, slate, wool and other goods from Llangollen to all parts of the country. A journey to Kent, for example, was possible and took over three weeks by horse drawn barge. The Llangollen section of canal was lucky to be powered by fresh water, and remained active long after others had fallen into decline. The railways were the biggest nails in the coffins of most of the canal companies, and the Ellesmere Canal Company was no exception. Further trouble loomed with increasing motorization following World War II, and canals all over the country which had long been in decline suffered severely.

The canal today, however, probably sees more traffic than it ever did, with a large number of pleasure boats on the water. Their journeys terminate at Wharf Hill, Llangollen, where there is a canal museum. Horse-drawn canal boat trips may be enjoyed from here during the summer, to the Horseshoe Falls and back or to the beautiful old Chainbridge Hotel, where the horse-drawn barge stops at the back door. The canal is also popular with anglers, having a variety of coarse fish and trout in it. When the section is drained, one question that is often asked is 'where does the water go?' The answer is quite simple; a draining plug is removed at Pontcysyllte and the water falls a hundred feet, back into the river whence it came.

Fresh water or not, the coming of the railway heralded a steep decline for the sure but slow canals. The railway line through Llangollen soon became the main artery for goods from Ruabon to Y Bermo (Barmouth), and a journey from Llangollen to Kent by the newfangled railroad would certainly not take upwards of three weeks. The railways also had the benefit of being able to transport substantial and heavy commodities such as rock and slate just as efficiently as the waterways. In addition, this was one of the most beautiful lines in Britain, going to a very popular summer destination on the western seaside. Thus the summer traffic in humans was more or less ensured. The railway therefore enjoyed enormous success and survived until the inevitable Beeching axe severed it in the early sixties. It seems incongruous that, today, the Llangollen Railway Company has had to re-lay track so that a tourist service can be run westwards from Llangollen. The journey gets longer every few years as more and more track is re-laid, and hopefully soon the romantic smoke of the steam engine will once again reach as far as Corwen. As it is, the visitor may enjoy diesel or steam to pull them on this beautiful journey daily.

The biggest problem facing the new railway in Llangollen itself was the centuries old bridge across the Dee. The only solution was to apply for permission to cut through part of the bridge and, in doing so, creating an extra arch.

The town bridge that crosses the Dee is one of the 'Seven Wonders of Wales', as noted in the old rhyme:

*Pistyll Rhaeadr and Wrexham steeple,*
*Snowdon's mountain without its people,*
*Overton yew-trees, St Winifred wells,*
*Llangollen Bridge and Gresford bells.*

It is claimed to be the oldest stone bridge in Wales, first built, supposedly, by .Dr John Trefor, Bishop of St Asaph in 1346. It was then only the width of a horse-cart, but has of course been altered and widened many times since. In 1992/3 it was again re-supported so as to comply with EEC regulations which ensure that all bridges intended to carry HGV's of forty tons or more are sound. Today only four of the five arches are open, the fifth arch which was created for the old railway track having been re-filled. Houses have since been built on the old railway line on the Ruabon side of the bridge.

In the town centre of Llangollen, just off the main street, is the very beautiful 12th century (originally) Parish Church of St Collen. The ceiling is beautifully carved, and the door to the Choir vestry is from the 14th century. The church has been enlarged and considerably repaired in its time.

Another interesting church can be seen by taking the canal-boat, or walking the towpath, to Llantysilio. It must be one of the most attractive churches in the whole of Wales, set on the banks of the river Dee (Afon Dyfrdwy). The present building comes from the 15th century, having undergone major restoration in 1869. It still retains much of its original 15th century glass, and has part of an earlier 12th century building incorporated into it. The church can also be reached by leaving the A542 at Pentrefelin and following the B5103 Llantysilio road. The church will then be on your left.

The main attraction to Llangollen is undoubtedly the International Eisteddfod. Held annually during July since its inception in 1947, it has succeeded in what it was designed to do, and still does so year after year. There grew a feeling in this small town that something was needed to bring the peoples of the world together again following the harrowing and divisive years of the Second World War. The Eisteddfod idea in itself was an inspiration, for what better way is there to unite than by giving the peoples of nations, large and small, the opportunity to demonstrate and to experience the diversity of their own and other cultures. For the week long festival, Llangollen becomes a cauldron of nations where singers from the arctic circle mingle with Patagonian Welsh speaking flamenco guitarists, and bare-breasted African dancers of both sexes mingle with male voice choirs from such places as Colne, Saskatchewan and Froncysyllte. The new pavilion that houses the main cultural activities, which has caused controversy but is highly acclaimed by those who use it, stands in a field between the canal and the A542. However, impromptu performances are apt to break out anywhere between the Eisteddfod field and the centre of town, with the old bridge being a favourite gathering point.

Llangollen is also a legendary fishing centre, offering coarse fishing in the canal and game fishing in the Dee. Mainly famous for its wonderful salmon, the river enjoys good support from all over the world. The World International Fly-Fishing Championships of 1990 were held on the Dee, based at Llangollen, with great success.

In an attempt to assist the salmon through the Llangollen town area of the Dee, where many fish were taken by poachers after the last war, the then River Authority blew-up several weirs. This encouraged the fish upstream since it prevented them shoaling in the shallows downstream of the weir, where they could so easily be reached with a gaff by poachers. Fish were, of course, much more plentiful in those halcyon days.

I remember as a lad, waiting for a bus home to Mold one summer's night, seeing Major Douglas Jones fishing his water below the old Llangollen mill. Having time to spare, I joined him. He told me how in 1946, during one day from that very pool, he took forty-six salmon before stopping, tired from playing the fish, and not because the fish had suddenly run out. Another man told me that, from the next pool downstream, his father had taken twenty-eight salmon, and laid them out on the pantry floor. He had then beaten his son until he couldn't walk so that he didn't tell anybody about the fish, having wandered into the pantry and seen the spectacle.

But sporting fish, especially the salmon population, in the Dee is in serious decline. Netting by commercial trawlers in the Irish Sea is taking a huge toll, and it seems that nobody truly cares about conservation. Any fish caught in a net off Ireland, which is programmed by birth to return to spawn in the Dee, is lost, and the future of a whole species is under threat. The situation is improving somewhat since the reduction in the number of nets on the estuary, but it is early days yet to be certain that the trend is up.

Anglers wishing to fish at Llangollen may purchase tickets for the Dee from the newsagent in Chapel Street, as well as association maps of the water and rules. Tickets are available for salmon and trout, with grayling being restricted to members in wintertime. All the fishing is controlled by the Llangollen Angling Association that today has assets in excess of £2 million from a start of just over £1.00. It is mostly fly-only for trout, and cannot be bettered anywhere.

George Borrow mentioned the fishing in Llangollen in *Wild Wales*. The idea of a local fishing association was unheard of then, all sporting rights being in the hands of absentee landlords. And it seems that Russian aristocrats had far more chance of a legal day's fishing on the Dee than the people who had lived on her banks throughout their lives. This was true of course of all such 'sport' around Llangollen. Rich families such as the Mostyns, the Williams-Wynns and the Myddletons had all rights to the native grouse on the high ground, although they would probably only visit that high ground for a day or two every year so that they may shoot a few birds in distinguished company. Pheasants were raised by gamekeepers for these people, again for the pleasure of being shot by people with distinguished double-barrels. The grouse, like the salmon, is now in decline, but more pheasants are reared in the area around Llangollen than ever.

In autumn after the salmon season has ended (October 17th) International Canoe Championships are held on the Dee at Llangollen and they are a marvellous spectacle as the canoeist fights the white water just below Llangollen Bridge. The bridges are usually crowded with the public as well as photographers who have an excellent view of proceedings, and can stay bone-dry as well.

Employment around Llangollen is largely limited to work that is related to agriculture, although a good few are employed at the massive nearby Monsanto Chemical Works. Chirk also has a few small factories, which helps. One big employer in the town used to be the Llangollen Hide & Skin Company, which collected and tanned hides until it was bought-out in 1990 and promptly closed down. It had been an employer for well over one hundred years and was noted for high-class leather goods. Obviously there is a good deal of seasonal tourist related employment, but this is largely confined to the summer months.

Law and order are well represented here - the Police Station and Courthouse is an attractive building in itself, just off the main street. The records kept there include the sad tale of a man who was tried and hanged for the crime of stealing a sheep to feed his family. None of the people who 'legally' stole the land, through Acts of Parliament, on which the sheep probably grazed are mentioned in the lists of those tried, let alone hung. They would probably have sat in judgement though, when the *werin* were sent to hang or deported for much lesser crimes. George

Borrow mentions a barber's pole stuck in the ground just off the A5, and relates what he discovered on making enquiries. It seemed that a local barber had cruelly killed his wife and was hanged at that very spot, the pole being left as a reminder to others of his fate. There was also a considerable oak tree on the A5 near Llangollen where, in the days of the stagecoach, they hanged people who were convicted of robbing the mail-coach. It was sited near a regular robbing-point, and it was the policy then to hang people as near to the scene of their crime as possible.

Overlooking Llangollen from the south is Plas Newydd, an attractive and large black and white building. From 1780 until 1831, this was the home of Lady Eleanor Butler and Miss Sarah Ponsonby, two spinsters who became known as 'The Ladies of Llangollen'. Their remains remain in Llangollen churchyard.

That they were eccentric goes without saying – people of most ilks frowned upon two ladies sleeping in the same bed. But despite their undoubted eccentric attitude to life and their solitary existence, they did draw famous people to Plas Newydd, including Lord Byron, George Canning, Lord Castlereagh, the Duke of Gloucester, William Wordsworth and the Duke of Wellington. It was said of them that they made excellent company and that good quality conversation was to be had in their presence. They apparently chose to keep themselves very much to themselves, bothering little with other people, unless they were famous or of distinguished blood, seemingly.

Lady Butler was herself from a distinguished Catholic family in Ireland and was related to the Duke of Ormonde. Sarah Ponsonby was from a more impoverished family, the history of which was not distinguished enough to survive the passage of the years, apart from the fact that her grandfather was a distinguished General. They met in Kilkenny whilst at school, Sarah then was only 13 years old and Lady Eleanor 29. A romantic friendship ensued and they ran away together from Ireland, but were apprehended by their parents. On the second attempt to run away, they made it to Llangollen and bought a small property called Pen-y-maes. This was enlarged and became known as Plas Newydd. It is open to public viewing in summer.

In 1818 a Mr H G Steele took a tour of North Wales and wrote down his account of his travels. He met the two ladies from Plas Newydd and described their undying love for each other; saying that they 'resolved never to disunite each other, to live and die together; to sojourn in some secluded spot remote from tumult, gaiety and bustle'. He continues that 'Lady Eleanor and Miss Ponsonby are never seen either at home or abroad attired in any other ... than Riding habit; their hair dressed and powdered, in every respect resembling the Man of Fashion as far as respects dress'. The ladies had a gardener who had instructions to show visitors over the property including the house itself, which had a remarkable collection of books. The gardens were also noted for their plants.

During his stay at Llangollen, he mentions that his little guesthouse served stewed eels and small roast ducks, and that after a meal they were entertained by a harpist. Llangollen was at that time, he tells us, noted for its eels, with many being caught in the Dee and sold in other towns. The town was also noted for its high-quality poultry, of which there was plenty in the markets. Steele also records that Llangollen then had 289 houses and 1287 inhabitants

There are many miles of excellent walks above Llangollen in the hills. All the footpaths are marked on the relevant OS maps, and most are adequately sign-posted. It is well worth noting, however, that farmers on the heather covered hilltops frequently discover the remains of bombs and incendiary bombs. In the dark days of the last World War, these mountains were set alight so as to attract German bombers on their way to Liverpool, by making them think that the fires were Liverpool burning. The idea was that they dropped their bombs here, thus causing little damage. Many bombs failed to explode on impact and remain partially hidden in the heather and bog of the uplands. They should never, under any circumstances, be touched.

One night during the hot summer of 1976, I was fly-fishing for sea trout in the Dee. The surrounding hills were alight because of gorse fires, and there was a terrible loss of wildlife because the blaze engulfed forestry as well as moorland. So fierce was the firelight that I was able to change my flies without the aid of my small torch. I was later told that many of the older people had vivid flashbacks to the dark days of war, and that many a memory burned fully that night. I also saw a huge ball of fire crashing down the mountainside, complete with an explosion, and I assumed it to be an unexploded wartime bomb. But next day I was to learn that a Fire Service Landrover had overturned, throwing its crew out, before crashing down the mountain. Thankfully nobody was seriously hurt. Dawn the next morning highlighted the spectacular blaze with an enormous orange and red glow, as the fearsome rising sun and the mountain fires illuminated the entire eastern skyline. It was a strange night, one that I am unlikely to forget in a hurry.

Llangollen excels at hospitality. Bed and breakfast is plentiful and the Welsh Tourist Board will assist in finding places. The hills above the town offer an abundance of wildlife to watch; red and black grouse, buzzards, peregrine falcons, merlins, harriers as well as a host of other birds. There is a canoeing school by the A5, at the former Deeside-Broadhursts's Steel Stockists factory, which was before that the Mile-end mill.

When I first went to Llangollen in the 1950's, the town's cattle market was still operating and all the trains on the Ruabon/ Y Bermo line were steamers. There was still the odd pony and trap in use. The place had a distinct hint of George Borrow about it. Thankfully much remains, due to its setting and its strict planning control, and Llangollen will never see the massive housing estates that have blighted so many beautiful Welsh towns in the past. And if Telford were able to pay a visit, I am sure that he would be pleased to see his canal as busy as ever.

# Holt

The Romans called Holt *Bovium;* the extensive clay deposits coupled with the sand and gravel drawing them here. The river was also a useful means of transportation. Having found such ideal conditions, the Romans set about building a huge tile factory that extended over twenty acres of land. Two workshops, built of stone and each over 30 metres long, have been identified. The barracks that housed workers, slaves etc. was in itself over 100 metres long. There were nine kilns on the site, one of which was of an unusual double flue design. Much tile-making equipment has also been unearthed.

The goods were taken downstream by boat from Holt, possibly to Heronbridge, and from there to Chester (*Deva*) by bullock (or horse) and cart. It has been suggested that flat-bottomed boats, of a type used by the Romans in other parts of Europe, were used. It is interesting that, until quite recently, flat bottomed cargo vessels were used from ports such as Connah's Quay, Mostyn and Point-of-Air to take goods around Hilbre Island to Liverpool or Birkenhead, towed by steam or sail powered vessels.

The Dee's course has altered considerably since the time of the Romans. Flood control schemes following World War II altered the course of the river as well as deepening it by the steep anti-flood banking that the Water Authority erected.

Remains of the Roman site of Bovium can be seen today, with access from the stile on the Holt-Farndon bridge.

On the banks of the Dee, to the south of Holt, is the town of Bangor Is-coed (Bangor-on-Dee). Around the year 616, Ethelfrith, the first king of Northumbria, a pagan, attacked and slayed all the monks from a large monastery at Bangor Is-coed. Numbers vary but Bede, who was apt to exaggerate about such things, said that 1200 monks died. The reason given for their being killed was that they fought with, of all deadly weapons, prayers. The monks had attempted to flee to Basingwerk Abbey but somewhere in the woods between Bangor-on-Dee and Holt, they were overtaken and bloodily killed. Recently, a farming friend and his son, who live off Hugmore Lane at Llanypwll, related a strange tale. On some nights, whilst attending to cows calving in the fields, they have heard screams and sighs. Others say that they have heard the same screams over many years, and it has been claimed that they are listening to the cries of the hunted monks, echoing down the centuries.

Holt escaped mention in the Doomsday Book, but Edward I had a new bridge built here to enable his army to cross into Wales. There may have been a wooden bridge there prior to this. There may also have been a bridge there during Roman times when a road may have ran from the area of the tile factory, through where Farndon Church now stands.

The bridge that was built for Edward's army was the site of a very dastardly deed in 1277. Madog Fychan was in possession of Castell Dinas Brân above Llangollen, and died in defence of his lofty position. His wife and two very young sons, Llywelyn and Gruffudd, survived him. The boys were placed under the control of the Lords Warren and Mortimer, two gentlemen who took their wards under Holt Bridge and there drowned them. Their bodies were hidden beneath one of the arches. Warren and Mortimer then shared the spoils with Warren securing Castell Dinas Brân for himself.

The present bridge is thought to date from the 15th century. It had a small chapel built on it, thus naming one of the arches 'The Lady's Arch'. Folklore has it that the bodies of the two young boys were concealed under this arch.

The Normans also built a castle at Holt, probably soon after the completion of the bridge. It was a useful position, being on the 'wrong side' of the Dee as far as the defending Welsh were concerned. The castle was described by Thomas Seymour, a one time occupant, as being 'of considerable strength and a formidable building, surrounded by a moat and a great fortress'.

John Norden recorded in 1620 that Holt Castle was in a 'ruinous condition', but contemporary sketches show that the main tower, moat and draw-bridge were in an excellent state of repair, as were the ramparts. The castle was, indeed, of considerable military importance during the Civil War, changing several times between Royalist and Parliamentarian hands. The Parliamentarians made a determined effort to take the whole of northern Wales in November 1643. A well-armed party moved crossed the Dee into Wales at Holt and an attack was made on Holt Castle. The occupants, fearing that the Parliamentarians had explosives, surrendered.

By the 18th of November, however, Royalist troops had arrived at Mostyn docks from Ireland, under Sir Roger Mostyn of Mostyn Castle. The Parliamentarian commanders Brereton and Myddleton, on hearing the news, moved their own troops back into England over Holt Bridge. Had Brereton and Myddleton known, most of the Irish were down with illness or seasickness, and unable to move let alone fight. It took a further two years for the Parliamentarians to gain full control of north-eastern Wales, but this time with the exception of Holt Castle. The defenders were well prepared and equipped, and so ensued a siege that lasted over twelve months.

Finally on January 13, 1647 Sir Richard Lloyd, who was defending, made a deal and surrendered the castle, bringing Holt's involvement in the Civil War to an end. Sir Richard, in return for agreeing to surrender, received £300 to travel abroad and a further £300 per year to maintain himself and his wife.

Following the Civil War, Holt Castle was ordered by Parliament to be slighted, and it was never occupied again. Further damage was inflicted in the 1870's when the Grosvenors of Eaton removed most of the castle to build Eaton Hall. The stone was moved by boat on the Dee, the Duke having a special flat-bottomed boat constructed for the job. Having completed its task, it was sunk downstream of Holt Bridge, and is still there, buried in the silt.

Just upstream of the remains of Holt Castle a new bridge has been constructed as part of the Holt/Farndon by-pass. Traffic is now diverted from the centre of Holt and Farndon, and the famous old bridge is now controlled by traffic lights.

St Chads Church, in the centre of Holt, is dedicated to the first Bishop of Lichfield. Like many other churches in Wales, it suffered much damage from pillage and looting during the English Civil War when all the parish records were destroyed. With them went much information about the early life of the church as well as Holt itself.

During the Civil War a single bell known as the 'Pancake Bell' was tolled to warn of impending attack from the Cheshire side of the river. Experts believe that the same bell hangs in the tower today. Whatever the truth, it continues to ring every Shrove Tuesday to remind people that it is Pancake Day.

# Heronbridge

Travelling downstream on the Dee, the next site of interest is Heronbridge. Its first recorded history comes from the Romans, who occupied it from the first until the early fourth century. Suggestions have also been made that people probably occupied the site long before the Romans came.

Excavations on the site show the remains of a short canal that the Romans cut, probably the first one in the isles of Britain. Its purpose was to link the main river Dee to what may have been the dock from which the tiles and pottery were off-loaded onto carts, so as to avoid the weir at Chester. It is thought that the dock was dedicated to the goddess *Minerva*.

Prof. F H Thompson in his excellent books thinks that this was also the site of a large bronze-smith as the entire site was equipped for a foundry. On-site excavations showed just one XXth Legion stamp which tends to suggest that this may have been a civilian rather than a military site, being two miles from *Deva* (Chester). Coal and grain deposits were found here, but they may have been from a later occupation. It is known that the Romans were amused by the glowing properties of lit coal.

Heronbridge today is nothing more than a grassy field with depressions in it, thus offering very little to the general layman.


# Chester

Romans and Royalists dominate the history of Chester. It is interesting that the first recorded drowning in the Dee was of a Roman officer who fell from a fishing boat while awaiting promotion (details can be found on a stone in Chester Museum). And possibly the first death due to the Civil War was also at Chester, when a soldier fell mortally wounded just outside the Eastgate.

There are tales about the ghosts of Roman soldiers patrolling the city walls of Chester at night. I haven't seen any myself but, if they do exist, they wouldn't look out of place. Invading armies still come to Chester, now armed with credit cards and cameras rather than spears. Unfortunately, one must take the rough with the smooth, because the seemingly endless hordes of tourists are having a seriously detrimental effect on the ancient paths and walkways of the city, especially the famous *Rows*. But Chester continues to draw people by the hundreds of thousands because it is a fascinating city.

Tourists who visit Chester will find a wealth of maps, tours and guides readily available from the Town Hall, including informative and relaxed bus tours. The city archives office – open to the public in the day – is in the same area, being part of the former Chester City Police Station and Courthouse.

\* \* \*

## The Romans at *Deva*

People had lived in the British Isles for ten thousand years and more, without break, before Tacitus mentioned the first Roman on the island in 48AD. The Celts were well established in the island a thousand years before Christ, coming from mainland Europe. Roman historians noted that the area from Afon Clwyd (river) to the Dee was the territory of the *Deceangli*; the area immediately to the south was the territory of the *Ordovices*; and the area from the Wirral to the far north was the territory of the *Brigantes*. Who, or whether any of them, lived in Chester has not been established, but the position of Chester within the Roman plan becomes clear. A strong fort on the Dee would separate the *Brigantes* from the *Decanglii* and *Ordovices* of northern Wales. In the same way, a fort at *Isca* (Caerleon) on the Wye would separate the *Dumnonii* of Devon and Cornwall, and the other tribes of southern England, from the *Silures* and *Demetae* of southern Wales.

The Romans were active in northern Wales at an early date; Tacitus described their attack on the all-important druidic centre of Ynys Môn (Anglesey) in 60AD. They understood that by ending the influence of the druids, they would be taking an enormous step towards ending the resistance of the Brythonic peoples. The earliest Roman gravestone in the Chester area is dated 80 AD and an accurate date for their establishment here would probably be about 75 AD.

*Deva* first became home to the *Legio II Aduitrix* (2nd Auxiliary Legion). After moving into Chester, they received the honour *Pia Fidelis* (the Loyal and Faithful) from the Emperor Vespasian (69-79AD), founder of the *Flavian* dynasty who raised the *II Aduitrix* himself following the Roman Civil War of 69 AD. The men of the legion were from Yugoslavia and northern Italy.

The fortress they built was not big, being of wood with earthen ramparts. Domitician, the younger son of Vespian, withdrew the *II Aduitrix* around 87 AD, and they never returned. Much of their construction was left incomplete.

Following the battle for Actum in 30 AD, the *Legio XX* had been raised and was stationed on the Rhine. This was one of the armies involved in the initial invasion of Britain; they were later stationed at Colchester (*Camulodunum*) in Essex. Coupled with the might of the 14th Legion they took on *Bodicaea*, queen of the *Iceni* tribe in the midland area of England. Their success in battle earned the *Legio XX* the honour *Valeria Victrix* (the Brave and Victorious). Following some time at *Viroconium* (Wroxetor) they came to Chester and set about enlarging the fortress, replacing the initial woodwork with local stone (much of it quarried at Manley near Frodsham).

From recovered stones it appears that the men of the *Legio XX* (the 20th Legion) were from Yugoslavia, Spain, Italy and France. The enlarged fortress took up an area of just over 60 acres and it was in fact the biggest of the Roman fortresses at 24.5 hectares, whereas the usual site was some 20 hectares.

Around the year 125 AD there seems to have been a substantial reduction in the construction work at Chester. The main reason appears to have been the movement north of considerable numbers of troops to build Hadrian's Wall. There is evidence that the *Legio XX*, along with others, were active in that area. It was not until 165 AD that the troops returned to Chester.

It is possible that the first Roman fortress would have been centred around where Chester Castle stands today. The fortress itself was surrounded by deep ditches, which included the troop-ditches. Some of these were over two metres deep – easy enough to get into but very difficult to get out of, making the attacking troops easy prey for the defenders from the walls above. The gates of any fortress are always the weakest part. At *Deva* they would have been made of wood with a walkway across the top joining the two walls. A tower would have supported each side. The fortress itself took about four years to build and the total complement of staff, both military and civilian, would have been from 5,000-6,000 persons. Piped water came from Boughton to the fortress in 79 AD through a system of pipes and gullies.

During excavations at Chester Cathedral in the 19th century the remains of an altar and a statute to the god Apollo were discovered along with an area of tiled-floor, drains and coins. It is thought that the site of the cathedral was the site of the Roman hospital, but much of the Roman remains are buried under the cathedral, and it is highly unlikely that they will ever be unearthed.

*Deva* was without doubt a massive administrative centre, the area within its jurisdiction possibly reaching as far as Derbyshire and

Lancashire. There also appears to have been considerable troop movement from the fort to other parts. There was also a Roman mint situated here, and when deposits of clay were discovered upriver at *Bovium* (Holt), and lead downstream at Fflint, Chester was well positioned to control both sites.

The Roman amphitheatre was built outside the walls of the fortress and in its day seated over eight thousand people. The remains are preserved today just off John Street, overlooking the river Dee. Most of the remains however are now under the nearby church of St John.

Fitness is paramount to the fighting efficiency of any army and the Romans were fanatical in this respect. They had the close proximity of the Welsh mountains and lakes, and also the river Dee to help them in their training. Even the civilian staff were expected to attain a high standard of fitness and were sent out on training sessions to ensure that standard was always maintained. If a fortress came under attack, the civilians were as vulnerable as the military staff, and to defend themselves, they were expected to be fit.

Roman life in occupied areas was not the one of luxury, eating, drinking and the delectable pleasures of the flesh that have been portrayed by film makers. There were few pleasures in patrolling the area of Trawsfynydd (Tomen-y-Mur) or Caernarfon (*Segontium*) or the Dee estuary in the depths of bitter Welsh winters. Many of the legionaries were, after all, from much warmer climes.

For the ordinary common soldier – the backbone of the army – life was somewhat bittersweet. The officer-class was entitled to a supply of fresh meat and the discovery of bones suggest that this supply was more than adequate. The common foot soldier had to make-do with gruel or porridge mostly, some other dairy based products, and fruit would also have been available. At Chester the supply of migratory fish was considerable with far more salmon and sea trout than the runs we experience today. The Romans were captivated by the flashing beauty of the salmon and gave it its generic name *Salmo*, meaning the leaper. Its full generic name is *Salmo-Salar*.

The Roman attitude towards the dead is fascinating. With the exception of children, the dead were buried outside the walls of the fortress. The children were buried wherever the father so desired, inside or outside: it was his choice as a grieving parent. There are graveyards outside Chester walls as in all places of Roman occupation. Thomas Hughes wrote in the year 1858 that, while cutting a railway siding off the Chester-Holyhead line into a field (known locally as *Lady Barrow Hey* or *Barrow Field*), several graves were opened and many were lined with tiles made at *Bovium*. Some had terracotta lamps (an emblem of immortality) and some had bronze lamps. In one grave the body of a lady of some distinction was found, covered in expensive jewellery, including diamond earrings and emeralds of excellent quality.

Hughes was also present at another exhumation in the area of Hough Green, where the remains of a Roman soldier of some distinction was discovered. The body had a coin placed in its mouth from the reign of Atho.

This practise of placing a coin in the mouth of the departed was commonplace. Some coins were placed alongside the dead whilst others were laid in the body. The thinking was that the coin would pay Charon the Ferryman to take the departed across the rivers of the underworld to the realms of Hades. Sometimes coins were placed on the eyes of the dead to show their bodies at peace, and also to cover any toll costs.

Before the Christian era the Romans also practised cremation, the ashes being placed in vases that were then buried. Some vases were deliberately broken, the best explanation for this being that the family wanted to release the incarcerated from the vessel.

In the Handbridge area of Chester across the old Dee Bridge, which was from Roman times until quite recently the main way in and out of the city, substantial buried Roman remains have been discovered. The finds include both earth burial and cremated remains. The other main site was where the Chester Royal Infirmary now stands.

An intriguing practise of Roman burial, and not wholly understood, was that of placing hobnails in the grave. Several exhumations in this country have revealed this practise, a one-time explanation being that the nails were part of the wooden coffin but this is under serious review.

Chester was no different than elsewhere. In some graves it appears that quality boots were placed on the feet of the departed, with a more than adequate supply of nails placed alongside the feet presumably for use by the departed in the afterlife. At one find in Cirencester over 2,000 specially made hobnails were unearthed, and it is presumed that they were for use in burials.

Another unexplained practise of Roman burial was that of cutting the head, and sometimes the limbs, off the bodies. The head was then placed between the legs, and severed limbs placed at various locations about a body in other burials. The obvious conclusion is that this is the body of a criminal who was killed by decapitation, but scholars think this unlikely. The practise of carefully severing the limbs is not explained, but again the suggestion has been made that here lies an undesirable and that by severing the limbs, he or she would be rendered harmless in any after-life.

The Romans believed that the dead must lie undisturbed at all costs, but they removed gravestones to resupport part of the city walls. One suggestion is that the growth of Christianity was such in the 4th and 5th centuries that people opposed to the Romans may have removed the stones. The severing of limbs and heads was also common at the same time.

By 255 AD a large part of the 20th Legion had been deployed to other areas, notably the Rhine and the Danube delta, and it seems that they were not replaced at Chester. It took a further one hundred and fifty years before the clay factory at Holt came to an end, suggesting that the Romans had little to fear from the Brythonic people. The Romans left the island during the early years of the fifth century and the country fell into a far more turbulent period in its history. The Brython/Welsh have often been accused of fighting amongst themselves, and subsequently being unable to run their own affairs. What is too often overlooked is that they were, far more importantly, fighting constantly against a growing tide of Germanic invaders. Places such as Chester were largely deserted, as they were incongruous with the needs of the times.

## Chester under the Normans

When the Danes arrived here in 893-4, they described the place as 'a deserted city in the Wirral'. But during the time of Edward the Elder (928-939) a mint was founded in the city. Thus was it given a much-improved status as sea-trade increased once more and Chester again became a provincial centre for north-western England. The city traded with Ireland and also with Scandinavian countries. The area of Lower Bridge Street had a large Nordic population, with some of the places of worship dedicated to their own saints in a pattern that is similar to York. A Viking attack in about 980, however, totally devastated the city, and it needed to be almost totally rebuilt.

When the Normans arrived at Chester, the city already had a recorded history that stretched back a full millennium. Their arrival brought a new impetus to the history of Chester but they were not popular occupiers and, in 1068, Welshmen allied with Saxons to attack the Normans at Shrewsbury. There were also attacks nearer to Chester. This apparently disturbed the first Earl of Chester, who complained that he was being attacked by both his Saxon and Welsh enemies. Much damage was done to the city during 1070 when the Normans punished the population for Saxon action in the recently finished rebellion. Two hundred and five houses were burnt, some of them possibly to make way for the new

Chester Castle. The area prospered greatly, however, for many reasons. Norman barons had been given total autonomy in the March – a kind of *no mans land* running from Chester in the north to Caerleon in the south, which therefore separated England from Wales. The eastern boundary of this territory was strictly demarcated but, while the Norman King was able to absolve himself of any direct blame for infringement, the western border was left open and the Barons could set it as far west as they dared. They were by no means shrinking violets and certainly demonstrated this in their very aggressive treatment of the Welsh, as they pushed the Marcher border ever westwards until they finally reached Afon Conwy. They established castles, for the usual purely defensive motives of course, in Fflint and then Rhuddlan. They also taxed the newly occupied populace heavily thus attracting further wealth to the city of Chester. The occupiers also imported great ecclesiastical artisans to oversee and partake in the foundation of wonderful monasteries and churches in Chester. In addition, the port prospered and grew considerably during the next few hundred years.

**Chester as a Port**

There has been much traffic on the river Dee probably from pre-Roman times. This was greatly increased however towards the end of the first millennium when Chester became the naval centre from where the Saxon navy was deployed to carry out raids against Vikings and such in the Irish Sea. Shipyards also developed here to repair, and probably build new, ships. Records also show that Chester was the centre of a considerable trade in animal skins with Ireland.

By 1000, the emphasis of the naval base was defending against, and probably attacking, the Welsh. By the end of this century, with the Normans in charge, all movement of ships to and from Chester was under the control of the King. This was because of the number of smugglers in many seaports, including Chester.

By the Middle Ages, Chester was in full swing as a seaport. In the 12th century it had developed into a well known tanning centre, producing leather and other by-products, much of which was exported to Ireland. The last skin-yard closed in the city centre only in the 1970s, moving to a new industrial estate Typical of the time also is the cargo of the *Mary of St Malo* which, in 1468, consisted of knives, wine, iron, glass, resin and kerchiefs. Exports at this time are recorded as mainly raw and tanned hides, cloth, wool, pottery and grain..

By the start of the 16th century trade was beginning between the Manchester Mills and Chester. Cotton was sent to Spain, as well as vast amounts of pottery. The Spanish trade was much sought after and highly prized, and the port of Chester was booming on all tides.

The *Welsh Ports Book* makes a fascinating read, giving a clear insight into shipping on the Dee in the 17th century. In those times Chester was classed as being a Welsh port, being the third main port in Wales. The cargoes mostly listed are hides, barley, and cloth. Slates from north Wales were also exported through Chester, having been brought here from smaller Welsh wharves or ports. *Commerce with Chester* a report from 1630 lists the following as being items traded from and into the port of Chester:

'Hides, fish, salmon, hake, herrings. Irish Wool, linen, cloth, Marten skins and skins of Otters, squirrels, Irish Hares, of sheep, lambs, fox. Felles of sheepe, kiddes, and connies aplenty. Wines from an earlier period and flax, and slate, and cheese of course.'

But Chester as a port also had a bad reputation, to the extent that many traders preferred to avoid the area at all costs. It was also a notable place for the bad treatment of sailors who entered the port. Chester also figured in the convict and slave-trade, many people being sent directly from Chester, or sent to Liverpool from where they continued their enforced journey.

One convict ship was the *Success*. She was a large ship of 621 tons, and was raised from the bed of Sydney harbour sometime before World War 1. She sailed to Britain, coming up the Dee to Chester around 1914. It was said that this tourist attraction was the last big ship to come up the river as far as Chester. She stayed some time in Chester docks before moving on again.

The city's population was 6,000 in 1600. But the fact that Chester was a port caused much fluctuation in the figures with many seeking a living from the thriving export of livestock from Chester docks. In 1639 over 16,000 cattle and 2,000 sheep arrived on the Dee, compared to a total of just 2,000 on the Mersey. The English Civil War (1642-48) put paid to much of the trade, but matters improved quickly in later years. By 1666 the numbers rose to 16,000 cattle and 25,000 sheep with the Mersey having about a third of this. During the summer Irish drovers arrived with livestock and many sought work on the local Welsh farms, who in-turn rented grazing to the Irish livestock. These were moved on to bigger cities before the ferocious winters set in.

### Chester in the Civil War

It was quickly seen by Parliamentarians that Chester, the main trading port from the north-west with Ireland and closely connected through the

Dee to a Royalist northern Wales, should be secured as soon as possible. Charles I came to Chester on September 23rd, 1642 to watch, from what is now known as *King Charles Tower*, his army being soundly thrashed on Rowton Moor. He quickly left the city, going on to Holt, Wrexham and then Shrewsbury. Meanwhile, Sir Williams Brereton surrounded Chester with a show of strength of over twenty thousand men.

A siege was maintained until February 1646, when it was obvious that there was no further help to aid the city. The King was in no position to assist. Ireland had done her best as had Sir Roger Mostyn and, after a meeting of the officers and the realisation that not even a rat survived in the city to eat, a surrender was made to Brereton and the siege of the City of Chester was over.

The damage done to the city during the Civil War was immense. Randle Holmer (1627-99) writing of a visit to Chester following the war records that large parts of the city was destroyed by fire, and many of her fine timber buildings were lost in flames due to the relentless attacks. There was at this time a long row of properties that ran from outside the city walls from Lower Bridge Street to Handbridge. All were destroyed by fire. There had been severe grenade attacks on Watergate Street and not a property remained untouched to some degree. Most of the churches within the city, and the considerable stabling area, were considerably damaged.

Throughout most of the siege, the earlier part the city had received supplies of food, coal and ammunitions through the tenacity of Sir Roger Mostyn. But as his lines of communication were slowly strangled by Sir William Brereton's forces, the main road from north Wales through Hawarden was cut off, the river Dee was too dangerous to use, and the supplies slowly dwindled away to nothing.

This is in complete contrast to a written report by Henry Hastings (1586-1643) when he wrote of a visit to the city before the ravages of war. He praised the city for retaining so many fine timber buildings and mills on the Dee (at Handbridge). He writes of the ruinous condition of the castle and comments on the problems of shipping not being able to reach the city walls on most tides. This was affecting the increasing trade with Ireland from the city, in both people and cargoes. He note that much coal was being exported from Chester to Ireland.


## Ecclesiastical Chester

The first church in Chester, probably a wooden affair in the old Celtic Church tradition, was reputedly built in 660. Other churches followed, including one in 907 on the site of the present cathedral, which was dedicated to St Werburgh, daughter of the Mercian king Wulfere. She was a nun who died and was buried at Hanbury in Staffordshire. Her remains were moved to the church in Chester as a precaution against damage from the marauding Danes. Chester city walls were refortified at the same time, and the city was deemed a safer place to keep such precious relics.

Chester has had connections with various religious factions over the centuries. The Grey Friars (Franciscans) established a monastery in the Watergate area of the city, near the Linen Hall, during the reign of Henry III. The building remained intact until the middle of the 17th century. The Black Friars (Dominican) had a presence in the Nicholas Street area, whilst the White Friars (Carmelites) were established by Thomas Stadham in 1279 in the area that is still known as White Friars. Following the Dissolution of the Monasteries, Sir Thomas Egerton built a mansion here and on July 21st, 1597 the steeple of the old church was pulled down. It was described in writing as being 'of great height and beauty and the only sea-mark for the direction of Chester from the bar'.

The most famous landmark in the city, however, is probably its cathedral. Following the Norman Conquest Hugh Lupus, the Earl of Chester, wanted a Benedictine Abbey in Chester, and called upon Anslem the Abbot of Bec in Normandy to help him. Anslem arrived in Chester in 1092 accompanied by some monks, and they commenced the construction of an Abbey that was then attached to Lichfield Cathedral. It took over 150 years to complete. The abbey was built on the site of St Werburghs, and dedicated to the same Saint.

The Abbey was dissolved by Henry VIII in 1540, but converted into a Cathedral, thus saving it from destruction. It was newly dedicated as *The Cathedral Church of Christ and the Blessed Virgin Mary*.

By the end of the 18th century the soft sandstone was showing much wear and tear, and a hugely expensive improvement programme was commenced. The man who got repairs underway was Dean Anson (1839-67), followed by Dean Howson who had the expert assistance of Sir George Gilbert Scott between 1868 and 1876. Extensive work was done on both the interior and the exterior. Much of the original 1090 building remains, including the North Transept, part of the Cloisters, the Refectory and the Baptistery.

The cathedral has the only complete example of an ecclesiastical courtroom in England, and is still in use today. Following advice that ringing the ten bells in the main tower could cause extensive damage, a separate tower was constructed outside the cathedral in 1975, almost in the city walls. The organ was built in 1919 by William Hill and rebuilt in 1969-70 by Rushworth & Draper. Apart from some of the finest woodcarvings anywhere in Britain, Chester Cathedral also has an extensive library of old and rare books, which are faithfully restored by volunteers under the watchful eye of specialists. One of the rarest books in the cathedral is known as *Polychronicon* written by a monk of the old St Werburgh Abbey, called Ranulp Higden, in 1352. It is a history of the world from the creation.

St John's Church is close to the remains of the Roman Amphitheatre. The building is Norman and the stonework less weathered than the cathedral. It is said to have been built on the site of a 6th century church, and is an excellent example of Norman architecture with great internal columns that lean very slightly outwards, this being the only known example in England. It also contains 17th century paintings by the Holme family, some of whom were past Mayors of the City.

In the grounds of St John's are the ruins of another 11th century Norman church that was destroyed following the Dissolution. Part of it became a Parish church but eventually fell into disuse.

In the time of the Normans, St John's and St Werburgh's dominated Chester. In the Domesday Book, St John's was said to have a Dean and owned land both inside and outside the city. In 1075 it was taken over by Peter, the Norman Bishop of Lichfield. He was succeeded by Robert who is recorded in the Domesday Book as 'The Bishop of Chester'. There is a limited amount of evidence that Souter's Lane near St John's Church was, at one time, possibly a private inlet or small dock from the Dee to the church itself.

## Chester Castle

The remains of Chester Castle can be seen on the right as one enters the city having crossed the Grosvenor Bridge along the A483.

Founded in 1070, it was developed by several of the Marcher Barons who held Chester. In Norman times it was of the motte and bailey type. Between 1159 and 1160, the square tower was added and the inner bailey was reinforced. The surviving tower is the Agricola Tower (named after Julius Agricola, the Roman Governor), which is the gateway to the castle.

The last Marcher Earl, John the Scot, died in 1237 and the Earldom passed to the King, Henry III. This heralded a building operation to restore the city when stone was used to replace the castle's outer bailey. Edward, the elder son of Henry and the future Edward I, succeeded his father to the earldom in 1254, eighteen years before he became king.

Henry was unwilling to adhere to Magna Carta, formed between King John and the rebellious Barons in 1215, which might explain his reasoning in taking the earldom himself. The country was moving towards a Civil War and Chester anticipated problems, giving added impetus to the strengthening of the city and the castle. In March 1264 the Barons' leader Simon de Montfort, the King's brother in law, captured Henry at Lewes and went on to rule England for the next year. Henry however defeated the Barons at Eavesham, killing Montford in the process, in 1265.

Chester castle was always a base for campaigns in Wales. It also became a collecting point for master craftsmen who later worked on the castles of Edward I in north Wales.

In 1293 the outer gatehouse was built. In 1302 a fire badly damaged the castle and the Agricola Tower in particular. A number of inner buildings were destroyed. Once repaired it became the base for the famous Cheshire Archers (of whom most were Welsh).

During the 15th century trading in Chester eased quite considerably and the river began to silt heavily. The castle, which was then also a small port, was falling into a state of disrepair. In 1579 a major rebuilding programme was undertaken but in 1585 the main castle bridge collapsed.

The castle was also used as a prison, being one of the coldest and most inhumane anywhere in Britain. The Normans very cruelly held Gruffudd ap Cynan, Prince of Gwynedd, for some twelve years in a hole in the ground, until he escaped in 1094. In later times, prisoners had a roof, but it leaked and rain was said to 'run like a river through the prison'. A single prison room was used for male and female prisoners'. The conditions for women were atrocious with the male guards acting no better than the male prisoners. The building also housed the Assizes. Prisoners housed in the single room over the gateway were said to throw stones at the judges as they picked their way across the rickety old bridge into the castle. The prisoners then had to convince His Honour of their undoubted innocence in the matter he was hearing, as well as in the matter of endangering his life upon entering the castle.

The castle was also used as a mustering point for troops for Ireland. In the late 17th century William III used the castle as an embarkation point for many of his troops on their way to fight in Ireland.

The Jacobite Rebellions of 1715 and 1745 caused a considerable programme of work to repair the castle, which had become dilapidated. Its main purpose was to house prisoners from the rebellion, many of whom died from the cold, fever or lack of food.

Today, only a small part of the castle remains this being used as a military museum. The prison was demolished in 1877 but the castle did not come under the jurisdiction of the city of Chester until 1974.

## The Old Dee Bridge and the Weir at Chester

At the bottom of Lower Bridge Street is another of the entrances into the walled city – where the Old Dee Bridge crosses the river Dee. This was, until the 1850's, the only way into the city across the river. The Grosvenor Bridge was first built in 1852 and then rebuilt in 1923. It was then the largest single-span bridge in the world. This bridge crosses the Roodee or 'Rood-eye' as it is spelt in older manuals.

The first Old Dee Bridge was of wood. The Romans built it at this, the shallowest, crossing point on the Dee in the area. The fact that it was also a fording point may still be seen at low water.

The wood was later replaced by locally cut stone, and it has remained a bridge of immense value to the city ever since. Throughout its history, the bridge has been the focal point of any attack on the city. Today it is regulated by traffic lights, as the bridge is too narrow to allow vehicles to pass.

In 1093 Hugh Lupus, Earl of Chester gave authorisation for the construction of a corn-mill on this bridge, and a fulling-mill was built opposite. A fulling mill was fairly common on many major rivers in Britain. It is a mill where cloth was washed and thickened, at first by beating but latterly by rolling. In some parts, women trod the cloth in containers much the same as they do with grapes for wine.

By the 13th century the Crown had acquired the mill and in 1277 it was leased to a Master Richard. But problems arose concerning the weir just upstream of the mill. Part of this weir is natural, but man made additions were probably made from the 10th century. By the 13th century there were complaints about the flow of water, which affected the mill, and this led to claims that the Crown was responsible for its maintenance.

Many other problems were related to the weir including damage to the same mill in February 1601, putting it out of action for at least three months. There was also a flooding problem at Eaton that was partly attributed to the weir. Evidence given to Commissioners at an enquiry in 1608 claimed that the weir at Chester interfered considerably with shipping below the city, and that it also obstructed the passage of fish travelling upstream from the sea to their spawning grounds. The outcome of the enquiry was that part of the weir at Chester should be pulled down. The weir, however, stayed intact. Another attempt was made to remove the weir in 1646-48 following the Civil War, but this also failed.

In 1840 the engineer Robert Stephenson was called to look again at flooding problems at Eaton, and he concluded that the weir must go. But on appeal it was once again saved and, instead, consideration was given to building earth ramparts alongside the Dee to contain the flow in the main channel at times of high (storm) water. These ramparts are still in place today, and can be seen upstream of the suspension bridge at the Groves on the right-hand bank, looking upstream from the well-worn path through the meadows.

The *River Dee Fisheries Board* was formed in 1866, and under Acts of Parliament of 1861 and 1865 they had the brief to improve the river Dee as a fishery. It comprised of six members selected from the counties of Cheshire, Meirionnydd, Flintshire, Denbighshire and the City of Chester. But this body had limited powers and could in reality do little other than issue licences, employ bailiffs and develop the salmon hatcheries.

Below the weir in the race lay a salmon-trap that had been in place since the 16th century (and probably earlier). One of the mill-owners on the bridge wanted it removed but the miller at the opposite end claimed it would disrupt the flow to such an extent that his business would be seriously affected.

Again evidence was given to the Dee Fisheries Board by way of an enquiry, and the fish-trap was removed, but the mill-race left intact. The Board concluded that, on the Dee, there were mills at Pentrefelin (above Llangollen) Mile-end, Llangollen Town (upper Dee), Erbistock (middle), and Chester Weir (lower). The weir in Chester was the only one without a fish-pass and it was concluded that one should be installed.

A fish-pass was proposed and agreed upon in 1911 but its construction did not take place until 1919. This was modified and enlarged in the 1970's and can be seen on the extreme right hand of the river looking upstream, with the fish trapping house attached. This is used by fishery scientists to trap and tag (some by radio-tags) species of migratory fish so that their progress may be followed from the estuary upstream to their spawning grounds above Llangollen. From a fisherman or conservationist's point of view, the exercise has been most successful and valuable data has been obtained about much hitherto unknown behaviour of the migratory species (mostly salmon and sea-trout). Much remains unanswered, however, and will hopefully stay that way as this adds to the mystique of pursuing these species.

The current water authorities were formed following the severe drought of 1933-34, which focused political attention on the problems of supplying water to the large urban areas. The local water authority at Chester today abstract vast amounts of water near Eaton, with industry being the biggest user. Complaints are constantly made about this by a variety of pressure groups. It is claimed that the river has in effect become a two-tier system: from source to the abstraction plant at one level; and from the abstraction plant to the sea at a lower and slower level. This has often been cited as affecting the passage of fish upstream.

Today the weir still causes controversy. The National Rivers Authority has allowed canoeing by some schools on the weir and the fish-pass, which many see as a further hindrance to the declining fish stocks. But the weir seems safe, the general consensus being that removing it would cause more trouble than it would solve.

**Places of Interest in Chester City**

Chester is advertised as the 'walled city'. The visitor can gain access to the walls from several points around the city, via steps, and can then walk for a distance of over two miles in comfort. The walls are open 24 hours a day and make a very romantic moonlit stroll. The gateways to the city have been widened to cater for the ever-increasing size of vehicles, but a large part of the city centre is now traffic free for the convenience of pedestrians.

For accurate details of the city the visitor has a choice of visitors centre, the Grosvenor Museum (one of the country's finest) or the City Archive Office by the Town Hall.

The artist Louise Rayner has immortalised the famous 'Rows' and other locations in Chester. The paintings give an accurate view of life in the early 19th century as this highly sought artist sketched most of her work in the open streets, depicting how hard life was then within the walled city. Visitors frequently comment on the beauty of the city centre and the 'Rows' in particular.

The 'Rows' date back to the 13th century. Under some of the present day shops and stores, there are medieval cellars where wine and foodstuffs were stored in olden days. Louise Rayner's paintings clearly show that families, until well into the 19th or maybe even the 20th century, lived in the Rows. Today, no rooms in the 'Rows' are inhabited, shop space being at such a premium.

Visitors to the city are often struck by the lack of pubs and drinking houses in the centre, but this was not always the case. There are stories about drinking competitions, in the 1940's, where the competitors started at Chester Cross and walked down one side of the street towards the Boughton end (through Eastgate), drinking a half-pint of beer at each pub. They then returned up the other side of the street to the Cross, the winner being the least drunk, who had to prove his state by carrying out certain balancing acts. Not many survived.

The most photographed clock in Britain after 'Big Ben' in London is the Eastgate clock at Chester. Edward Evans-Lloyd, a citizen and Freeman, presented it to the city in 1897.

The Bear & Billet pub in Lower Bridge Street was built in 1664 and was owned by the Earl of Shrewsbury until the mid-9th century. There is a door in the gables through which goods were hoisted by pulley. The inn was said to have strong connections with the smuggling trade in days gone by.

Another well established public house is the Pied Bull in Upper Northgate Street which, in 1533, was home to the City Recorder. The present brick building dates from around 1654 when it became a coaching inn and the front was rebuilt. First called the Bull Mansions, it was here that George Borrow started his journey in 1854, and was bitterly disappointed when he receiving some disagreeable Cheshire cheese.

Slightly higher up is the Blue Bell, now a restaurant. This claims to have been built in 1494, and is said to be the oldest domestic building in the city. Both these properties would have been witness to the ravages of the Civil War.

The dominating Chester City Railway Station is one of the finest buildings of its type from the 19th century.

Chester Zoo, at Upton is the result of the work of one man, George Mottershead (1894-1978). He disliked seeing animals tied up in cages, and set about giving them as much freedom as he could. Chester Zoo is now the largest zoo in the north of Britain and is foremost in the fight for endangered species, many of which are bred at Chester.

Chester is ideally situated to tourism being in itself a fascinatingly historic place, and offers good access to Northern Wales and the North-west of England.


# Saltney Wharf

This was a railway company wharf. The main imported commodities were grain, manure, iron-ore, cement, scrap-iron while exports consisted mainly of minerals from Wales. Railway personnel staffed the port.

A fair amount of coal also passed through here, using the huge sidings that were alongside the port. Some of the sidings were in private hands, like those of Charles Randles who even had railway trucks with his name on the side.

The dock can be reached from Boundary Lane, which now leads to an industrial estate. There was until recently a knackers yard and animal by-products factory here that was notorious for its stench and smoke. Now that it is gone, Saltney has been able to enjoy a little prosperity, not to mention nice smelling air. Some World War II pillboxes can still be seen on the edge of the docks.

# Sandycroft Wharf

Sandycroft Iron Foundry owned this wharf that closed in 1926. It imported lead and iron for the foundry but, while it is likely that finished goods were exported through here, there are no records as such. Their iron grids for sewers and drains were well known and many are still in use today. This site also housed the Sandycroft Shipbuilders who built the 'Royal Charter'. Her keel was laid down adjacent to this factory in the spring of 1854 but her launch the following year was a calamitous affair. The ship was so large, and the Dee so narrow, that she had to be launched sideways, which was not a problem in itself. However, when she stopped halfway down the slipway, before a considerable crowd, there was much chest beating and talk about fate. It is thought that the wrong kind of grease had been used, thus causing friction that stopped the ship from slipping. But in retrospect of what happened to her off Anglesey on her fateful last journey, maybe the chest beaters had something to say on the matter after all.

All that remains of the Foundry wharf are a single basin with solid stone sides and the remains of the sluice gates from the now filled-in flushing-pool. There are also the remains of an old wooden landing stages, that was once a wharf for loading and unloading ships, mostly coal to Ireland. Erosion has destroyed the riverbank wharf frontage, and an anti-flood defence scheme by the National Rivers Authority that involved pulling-up the bank and placing tons of limestone rocks to prevent more erosion, has finished the job.

The site now supports several small units such as motor vehicle, supermarket trolley and electrical appliance repairers. Much of the original stone building has been taken down and replaced by steel buildings.

There isn't much to be seen now, but the site is reached along the B5129 Sandycroft road from Queensferry, turning left into the industrial estate and following the road to the old foundry site.

# Queensferry

The Dee was canalized here in 1737. After that time there were two ferrying services, the Higher Ferry at Saltney and the Lower Ferry at the point where the old Queensferry Bridge stands today. The river could also be forded here at low tide.

There was much shipbuilding here in the 1800s and the size of the docks grew accordingly. There was also a home for sailors' here, which was turned into a nonconformist chapel before being pulled down in the 1930s.

Joseph Turner built a chemical works here in the 1850s, and two landing stages for the plant. Gladstone, the Prime Minister who lived at Hawarden Castle, also built a single landing stage here. Nearby were several smaller wharves from which coal was exported from Aston colliery. This was brought down to the wharf on a small railway, and other small colliery owners from the Ewloe area also brought coal here for export, mostly to Ireland.

Queensferry also had an explosive works and wharf just upstream of the 'Old Ferry Bridge' from where explosives were exported. Any ship involved in loading or unloading explosives was required to hoist a red flag so that other ships could keep a safe distance until she was clear. The site later became a tar-works.

There was a good export trade in tiles and bricks from Northop and Buckley. The village also boasted a large fishing fleet, mostly catching herring, which was involved in the export trade, and ships came here from the Isle of Man to unload fish.

Queensferry's time of commercial sea faring came to an abrupt end following World War II although as a small boy I recall seeing a ship with a huge funnel tied-up at the wharf by the tar-works.

Travellers wishing to view the area can see most of what is left of the wooden wharves from the 'Old Ferry Bridge'. There is still a small factory on the site where the tar-works once stood. (See the canalization of the Dee and Lower Ferry for further information on Queensferry).

# Shotton Iron Works Wharves (John Summers & Sons)

John Summers ironworks came to Deeside in the 1890's and bought a huge area of reclaimed land for a reputed price of one shilling per acre. They then erected a highly profitable ironworks there, which later became a steelworks. Today it is a British Steel rolling mill for sheet metals.

John Summers had their own fleet of steamships, which were used to import raw materials and export iron and then steel. I can remember the ships from my childhood, towing flats that carried the cargo.

Summers were highly respected and enjoyed excellent relations with the other ports on the Dee. To ensure that this good will remain, they traded solely with the ironworks and declined offers to carry cargo for other ports.

This is one of the two docks that is operational on the Dee today and takes ships of up to 3,000 tons, mostly coming from Sweden to collect rolled steel. Ships can only come up the river on the bigger tides.

# Connah's Quay (late New Quay)

The first dock was built here in the 1740's following the canalization of the Dee, and was called New Quay. The dock was second only to Chester and, when Chester closed, it's trade moved to Connah's Quay and Mostyn. New Quay was the village's name in 1832, Connah's Quay referring only to the area immediately around the quay. While the family name Connah was well known in the area, it is unknown whether anyone of that name was directly connected to the development of the Quay.

It was discovered that, following subsidence of the main A548 in the 1960's near to the present entrance of Dock Road, the road was built over an old dock wall. It is thought that this was the original 18th century dock, or possibly part of a basin to serve the docks. The dock is reached along Dock Road (also marked 'Industrial Estate') from the A548. There was until the 1960's a considerable marshalling area for railway wagons here but this has now been built over. Two carthorses used to shunt the wagons until technology replaced them with a diesel shunter. Railway men, who took great pride in their horses and the state of the harness, staffed the yard.

The dock imported and exported a great variety of cargoes, but the main one was bricks and tiles from the Buckley area. A single line railway was installed from the main Wrexham-Bidston track, down through Buckley and Northop Hall, to the dock and the waiting ships. As a lad I often journeyed on the trains' footplate, during the last commercial years in the docks life.

The dock was a shipbuilding centre and there was also a ship-breakers yard here. When a ship came to be broken up, the practise was to remove as many saleable parts as possible, leaving the *bones* lying on the silt. The next ship was then floated on top of the old bones and the process repeated. Until quite recently, several *skeletons* could still be seen stacked one on top of each other, but the tides and the silts have now covered them.

Old photographs of the port show as many as six sailing-ships tied alongside each other at the quayside. Fights were common among captains vying for a berth. Sometimes, so many tied alongside that the main channel was blocked for shipping from upstream.

Two of the old docks have now been filled and the flushing pool has gone. The present dock remains but it is silted-up and useful only for the use of small fishing craft and privately owned boats. A decision to fill in the remaining dock was severely criticised and successfully fought against, and quite rightly so.

During the summer of 1991 a cockle-processing vessel from Holland arrived to collect cockles from the local fishermen. These fishermen had claimed for many years that discharges into the estuary from chemical factories in Fflint and Bagillt were destroying their industry. The factories refuted the claims but, since their closure, shellfish have again abounded here. As always, employment was deemed to be more important than the environment. The conservation of the species is still a mooted point, however, with the processing ship tied to the quay.

There is a wooden hut on the quay for the 'Quay Watermens Association'. They come and sit here in good weather to recall the days when they captained and worked as crew on ships out of the docks. The old gentlemen who come here are full of tales of the old docks, when up to a dozen ships would be out of the water receiving attention. They also tell tales about the dark days of World War II, when German aircraft flew over here on their way to bomb Liverpool, and how the ack-ack guns of Sealand aerodrome brought some down in the estuary. They will tell you of their prayers that Connah's Quay dock would be spared. One German bomber that was hit crash-landed into the silt just over the training wall. The crew was arrested, but the plane is still there today, buried in the silt.

They have many stories of ships coming home with holes in them from air-attacks, or from flying debris off other vessels. Planes discharged their explosive loads into the Dee off Fflint and Parkgate, and German submarines were seen in the mouth of the Dee. The whole line of the Dee estuary from Point-of-Air to Chester was one continuous line of industry at this time, mostly involved in working for the British war-machine. As such, they were all targets of the German offensive.

The Quay survived, however, and industry was able to breathe again after 1945. But Connah's Quay was losing out to Liverpool's bigger ships and, although it struggled on until the 1960's, it died a peaceful industrial death. Any hope of reviving the dock failed when the government sold-off the businesses that were by-products of British Steel. The brickworks at Northop Hall was one such casualty and, when the top and bottom yard closed, so did traffic on the single line.

A *Lifetime with Ships* by Tom Coppack remembers Connah's Quay through good and bad times. The Coppacks were an important family in the docks, and were there to the end.

Coppacks had bought several boats of their own to work out of Connah's Quay. One was the *Alice Linda*, 85 tons gross and registered at Chester. In 1913 whilst at anchor over Mostyn Deeps, she sank taking her captain J Garratt, who was asleep in his bunk, with her. The mate Ned Hughes was saved but divers recovered the body of the captain some time later.

The *Wrexham, Mold and Connah's Quay Railway Ports Registers* dated 1904 to 1922 show that 2,600 ships entered and left Connah's Quay docks. Most of the ships were schooners, but some were steamers of between 100 and 300 tons. Between January 2nd and May 7th 1905, 138 ships entered the port and the total weight of cargo handled was in excess of 20,000 tons.

The main coast railway was in many ways an asset to Connah's Quay docks, and improved their trade. Nevertheless the Railway Company sought to close the docks down and so force manufacturers to use the railway. In 1929 it was proposed that the dock should be closed and the Railway Company be relieved of all its obligations to carry on maintaining the dock. But Mr Coppack showed the enquiry that, since the Wrexham & Mold Railway Company had taken over control of the docks, the number of cranes had dropped from eight hand-cranes and five steam-cranes, to just two steam-cranes. Tonnage had fallen from a total of 58,281 tons in 1910 to 49,876 tons in 1911. He further stated that, owing to the inadequate facilities in the dock by 1928, the tonnage had fallen to only 11,067 tons. He maintained that the railway company was fully to blame, although they in reply blamed the poor conditions for shipping within the Dee for the decline in trade.

There was a great outcry from firms that were involved with the docks and shipping from as far afield as Derbyshire, the Midlands and Lancashire. The pressure of protest was so great that on February 6th 1930 the petition to close the docks was withdrawn. The dock survived and the Railway Company agreed to continue maintaining the cranes on the docks, provided that costs did not exceed £2,000 per annum. They also claimed that part of the old dock was unsafe, and the claim had to be agreed to by Mr Coppack and the objectors.

The old dock (of wooden construction) was therefore closed, resulting in fewer berths being available for ships enforcing them to tie-up alongside each other. This made loading and unloading a lengthy business, and involved considerable sums of money being paid in overtime so as to ensure that ships were away as soon as possible on the tide. There was a feeling that the Railway Company was allowing deterioration to set in on purpose and, by doing so, the wages of a crane-operator and a harbour-master would be saved.

The following is a reproduction of the port records, giving some indication of the trade that existed in Connah's Quay:

1894  457 vessels arrived at C'Quay and 302 left. Cargo mostly of bricks.
1904  313 vessels arrived and 181 left. Cargo mostly of bricks.
1910  Total goods imported and exported amounted to a total of 58,281 tons.
1911  Total goods was 49,816 tons.
1914  166 vessels arrived and 113 left.
1924  57 vessels arrived and 96 left (this was the period when the railway company was being obstructive).
1928  Total goods cargo was 11,064 tons.

In addition here are some details of the loads the ships carried, comparing two specific years:

|  | 1910 | 1928 |
| --- | --- | --- |
| Bricks | 30,511 tons | 9,179 tons |
| Manure | 4,417 tons | |
| Scrap | 5,950 tons | 124 tons |
| Pig Iron | 1,950 tons | 690 tons |
| Ore | 3,284 tons | |
| Grain | 5,710 tons | |
| Coal | 3,201 tons | 420 tons |
| Various Ores | 712 tons | |
| Chippings | 695 tons | |
| Clay | 709 tons | |
| Cement | 785 tons | |
| Pulp (wood) | 300 tons | |
| Leather | 20 tons | 14 tons |
| Timber | 117 tons | |
| Potatoes | | 100 tons |

This considerable drop in tonnage in 1928 was because the Railway Company tightened their grip. They also brought about a total of 43 new by-laws governing the docks that had to be strictly complied with. This led to the enquiry of 1929.

Two maps show that the dock changed little between 1771 and 1839. In 1865 a Mr Robert Roberts produced plans for a new dock. In 1860 the Railway Company acquired land adjacent to the docks, on the Chester side of the river and, some time after 1880, extended the dock on this side, which appears to have been the last extension.

The class of vessels using Connah's Quay port was usually small, with a draught of just 11-12 feet. From 1894 a new trade was founded with Norway, importing timber in large quantities.

A survivor of the port of Connah's Quay is the Schooner *Lizzie May*, which is preserved in Tiverton docks, Devon. She is now the property of the Maritime Trust, the intention being to preserve the ship as it is of such historical interest. Ferguson & Baird built the vessel at Connah's Quay in 1900 and named her *Lizzie May* after the two daughters of the owner, Captain John Coppack. Her first captain was Tom Hughes of Mold Road, Connah's Quay and she had a crew of five men. A wooden three-mast schooner with a 110 feet long beam; she was 23½ feet wide and could carry a cargo of 300 tons with a draught of 12 feet. Mr Robert Edwards & Sons, who had premises in Chapel Street, Connah's Quay, made the sails. Her main employment was transporting bricks from Connah's Quay to London. She also carried cement back to Deeside, and pitch from Queensferry.

In 1909 she was sold to Mr William Fleming of County Cork in Ireland and renamed the *Kathleen Mary* after his own daughters. He fitted her with an auxiliary engine and used her for coastal work around the Irish coasts. Some years later she passed into the hands of a Devon man and was registered at Bideford, her master at that time being Captain Jewell. She was in Liverpool in 1956-57 but lay derelict at Southampton by 1960.

In 1967 Captain Paul Hughes purchased her for just £2,800 and tried to raise a further £7,000 to make her seaworthy again, but failed. The Maritime Trust took over from there.

This is the only Connah's Quay built ship that has been preserved to my knowledge. Until they built the Quay Watermans Association hut on the dockside, there was an ex-Navy Corvette in the dock that the local sea-scouts and sailors used for practise and drills, but it has now been scrapped.

Just below Connah's Quay docks are the remains of the power station, built in the 1950's on 200 acres of reclaimed estuary land. It was quite an engineering feat, as the level of the marsh had to be raised by about eight feet. It involved dredging over three-quarters of a million tons of sand from the river, laying it on site, and then rolling it flat. Total cost was around £10,000,000. There was a huge marshalling yard linked to the nearby Chester-Holyhead railway line and very many tons of coal was brought here each year from local pits.

The power station is now closed and the cooling-towers were blown-up in 1993 in a spectacular display. Part of the site is now incorporated into the third crossing of the Dee.

The three ash-pit lagoons, which were part of the power station site, are now filled in. Most of this part of the works is given over to the Deeside Naturalists site, improvements having been made for the preservation of wildlife.

# Hawarden

This attractive village in the county of Fflint is known in Welsh as Penarlâg, the area being called this when the first church, attributed to St Deiniol, was supposedly built here in the 6th century. Deniol was the founder of the See of Bangor in 550, and died in 584. It is reputed that he is buried in Ynys Enlli (Bardsey) amidst about twenty thousand (Bede again) other saints.

The Dee was much closer to Hawarden Hill at the time, and the entire area of the Hawarden airfield and much of Mancot would have been part of a marsh that extended to the notorious Saltney marshes. The main route from Chester into northern Wales would have run roughly where it does today.

In 946 a Holy Cross or Rood apparently fell from the then church onto the Castellan's wife, and was promptly thrown into the Dee. It fetched up on a sandbank below Chester, the area thereafter being called the 'Rood-eye' which is now in the vicinity of Chester racecourse. There is another version that the Holy Rood was erected within Hawarden Parish Church. There had been a long drought and the villagers had long prayed for rain. When their prayers failed to be answered, they decided that the Holy Rood was no longer of value and threw it into the Dee below the village, to float to its sandbank near Chester..

The people of Chester were by then of Saxon blood. The blood of Penarlâg was Welsh. It was not a happy co-existence – there is an unrepealed by-law in Chester that a Welshman caught on the streets after dark may be lawfully killed. The good people of the church that was established at Roodee learnt of the Cross being thrown into the Dee at Penarlâg, and drew a similarity between the killing of Christ on the Cross, and the throwing of this cross into the river. This might be a reason why the good burghers of Chester called the *werin* of Penarlâg/Hawarden 'Jews' for a long time after. It might also be an indication of the tension between the two places.

The church at Haordine, as the compiler of the Doomsday Book spelt the village, went through a turbulent period following the coming of the Normans. Different factions of the Norman hierarchy disputed the tithe that went with the church, until it finally came into the hands of the rector of Hawarden Church. The church from that period enjoyed a long period of exclusivity, known as *Ecclesiastical Peculiar*, running its own affairs independently of the Bishops of St Asaph or Chester. In many respects, the rector of Hawarden acted like a bishop himself.

The church suffered greatly at the hands of Parliamentarian troops during the English Civil War (1642-1648), and its five bells were rung for a very long time following the Restoration. Six bells replaced the five in 1742.

The church went to court in the 18th century over who was responsible for the cost of burying the dead that were washed up on the shores of the Dee after shipwrecks. The Dee followed a twisted course from the estuary to Chester, and was dangerous to navigate. As a result many lives were lost. Hawarden used to pay the costs for both sides of the Dee, but these were high. The outcome of the case was that they paid only for their own side of the river.

The matter of the tithe was considerable. An indication of this can be had from 1778 when Hawarden received the rich crop-growing area of Saltney by Act of Parliament, the tithe then being valued at £3,286.

In 1810 the church bought its first organ for £248, and this was replaced in 1836. At the same time, hand-carved oak pews were installed in place of the benches. Other local churches installed pews much later.

It was not until 1849 that the church eventually came under the control of St Asaph. The rights of the rector, that had been considerable, disappeared. Records from the 15th and 16th centuries show that the rector held court over the people and was responsible for deciding upon the punishment. The penitent would either be received in the rectors' home in the presence of a churchwarden, or they would be clothed in a white shroud and walked to church, bare of head, feet and legs, on a Sunday. They then knelt before the altar and repeated parts of an oration, during which their 'sins' were announced, also to be repeated. Should they refuse to comply, they were excommunicated from the parish, or sent to prison. It has been recorded that one such offender – a Mary Davies – was actually buried late at night behind the church in an unmarked grave, and the burial is not recorded in the Parish Register.

In 1857 the church was broken into at the dead of the night, and two fires were started. The church was soon alight and a man was dispatched on horseback to Chester to summon help. According to a report in a Chester newspaper, four horses pulled the Chester City fire engine, which was in attendance within twenty minutes of receiving the call. Water was a problem, but a line of people with buckets managed to control the fire. The damage was extensive and much of the church was destroyed in the blaze. The total restoration cost was in excess of £8,000 but the money was raised. The Gladstones of Hawarden Castle were the main benefactors.

The first rector to have his name recorded at Hawarden was William de Montalt, in 1180. He came from the Norman family who built castles at Hawarden and Mold and also the church at Neston on the Wirral.

The graveyard has been enlarged twice, in 1860 and again in 1912, giving a burial area in excess of 4½ acres. Some of the older stonework bears marks suggesting that spears and swords were sharpened in the graveyard. This is connected with the thinking that any arm sharpened on a church stone would be more effective, as they were closer to God.

Next to the church is the splendid building that houses the library of St Deiniol. It was founded by W E Gladstone, the Liberal Prime Minister for 'The promotion of Divine learning' and contains 32,000 volumes, many of which were donated by Gladstone himself. The original building was of iron but following Gladstone's death, £10,000 was donated for a new more suitable building. The Duke of Westminster laid the foundation stone on October 5th 1899 and the building opened in October 1902. It is now a residential college for scholars and is open to the public on a daily basis.

The former Grammar school in Hawarden was founded by the church over 300 years ago to cater for all classes of people. The village also had three Dame schools.

Today all that remains of Hawarden Castle are a few stones. Who built the first castle here is not known, but the ditches are thought to be Bronze or Iron Age. Nothing has been found to suggest that the Romans used the site, but Hugh Lupus, the Norman Earl of Chester, built a motte and bailey castle here that was developed into a full Norman fort. Llywelyn ap Gruffudd destroyed this in 1265. Although it was decreed that another castle would not be built here, a report from 1282 reads: 'David's men went there by night to the castle at Hawardyn and there burned the house of the castle, while other did the same at Fflint'.

Hawarden Castle played its part in the English Civil War in supporting the King, even though it changed hands at least twice. In 1643, after a clever bit of trickery, it fell into the hands of the Parliamentarian troops along with the townships of Mold, Fflint and Holywell. This was overturned when 2.000 troops arrived at Mostyn from Ireland and marched for Chester in support of Charles I.

Brereton and Myddleton on hearing of troops approaching from Mostyn fled Hawarden but left a compliment of 120 men at the castle. The Irish surrounded the castle and, with the help of a Welsh contingent, prepared to wait. Further support came from Chester and the castle surrendered in December 1643. History has it that the inhabitants were shown little mercy by the Welsh soldiers, for this place had long been a thorn in Welsh sides. Back in Royalist hands the castle held out again until March 1646 when, with the King's permission, it surrendered. After the Civil War it was decimated as were many other Welsh castles.

Hawarden's most famous resident was William Ewart Gladstone (1809-1898). He was the son of a rich merchant and entered politics as a Tory in 1833, having been educated at Eton and Oxford. He was President of the Board of Trade under Peel between 1843 and 1845, but became a Liberal after leaving the Tories in 1846. He was a Liberal Prime Minister in 1868-74, 1880-85 and 1886, and again in 1892-94. He was a great reformer and lived at a time when social reform was a very important issue. He is buried in Westminster Abbey, London

# Ewloe Castle

The ruins of Ewloe Castle are accessible along the B5125 from the A55 at the Ewloe interchange. The entrance to the ruin is sign-posted from a lay-by, across some fields and then into a small woodland wherein the castle lies. Vehicles have to be left on the B5125.

Today the castle is well inland and appears to have no connection with the Dee. But a study of the river's route in the pre-1740 era, when it was canalized, shows that it ran further inland than it does today. Also, Wepre Brook that runs close to the castle, and is now just a trickle in summer, was then considerably bigger and a flat-bottomed boat might be floated down it into the Dee. There is some evidence that this might be the case as recently as World War I, when rowing-boats might get a fair distance from the Dee.

The name Ewloe is thought to have originated from the days of King Offa when the dyke separated Wales from England. The first castle here was established by Owain Gwynedd, one of the most successful leaders of the royal house of Gwynedd. It was probably of a motte and bailey style and made of wood, possibly with some stone in its construction.

By the time of Edward I, Ewloe had ceased to be of any militarily significance, and was in such a poor state of repair that he ignored it as being a possible site.

An account by one John Woods of Hawarden from 1540 is of interest. It stated that 'he knoweth Ewlow Common and Ewlow Woods well . . . but at this tyme . . . there was neither wood nor tymber herein . . . the castle is now so ruined and not anything standing but a small parcel of the south wall about three yards high and in length about some eight yards.'

This appears to be the last written record of Ewloe Castle until 1922, when the then Flintshire County Council sent workmen to tidy the place up and to remove the extensive ivy which had taken it over. From accounts, it seems that nothing had changed since Woods's time. Soon after, an Act of Parliament joined the Parish of Hawarden to the County of Fflint, when the castle and surrounding land came under the control of one of the Lords of Mold, Mr P T Davies-Cooke of Gwysaney Hall.

Ewloe Castle is now in the hands of the Department of the Environment and is looked after by CADW. It is situated in beautiful woodland and is a desirable place to visit any time of the year for any one looking for peace and quiet.

# Fflint

The Romans built a smelting plant at Pentre Ffwrn-dân (Village of the Fiery Furnace), which is often shortened to Pentre, but the site was probably occupied before the Romans discovered the rich vein of lead running from their fortress at Prestatyn through to Halkyn in the hills. It was there that they started their mining operations but nothing remains today of the Roman workings at Halkyn. All the information gleaned about Roman mining activities in the area has been from excavations on the Pentre site.

The Roman army oversaw the Halkyn mines with the labouring being done by slaves, probably in appalling conditions. Once the lead was mined, it was taken by pack animal to the foreshore and on to the Pentre site to be refined. It was then shipped from the docks that the Romans built at Pentre, or taken to Chester and exported from there with other goods.

The Pentre Ffwrn-dân site was large and well laid-out, and came into being between 69 and 96 AD. Excavations in the 1920's showed the remains of furnaces, grain and tools on site. In 1967 buildings were discovered and, from their design, it has been suggested that the Pentre site was dual-purpose with military officials being in attendance. Graves have also been found showing that the bodies were buried in coffins. The remains of coffin sealing nails have been found, and some of the graves were lined in Hawarden sandstone. Remains of a farm building from the period 138-193 AD have also been found. The site lay on the main Roman coastal route from *Segontium* (Caernarfon) to Prestatyn and *Deva* (Chester).

Nash-Williams in his book *The Roman Frontier in Wales* (1969) suggests that the Romans had considerable trouble subduing local people in the Fflint area. It is possible that the Pentre site was dual-purpose for this reason, but no fortress has yet been discovered nearby. Finds from the last excavations in the 1970's suggest that the quality of the houses was very high here. Some houses had pipes and baths, which might mean that officers used them.

Much of the lead was sent to Chester after it had been stamped with the distinctive Pentre stamp. Some of the pigs of lead made here have been found in Runcorn and all over Chester. One discovered in Shropshire weighed 134 lbs. and measured 23½ x 5½ inches and was 3½ inches thick. Another, discovered on the Roodeye site and displayed at Chester Museum, weighed over 190 lbs.

Pentre was occupied by the Romans until after 200 AD, when there was a slow but positive withdrawal of men and troops from Britain. The site then fell into decline and was vandalised during Norman times.

Lead was mined at Halkyn until World War I, this being the richest vein in Flintshire. In 1856 there were as many as thirty-nine mines operating the vein. After 1918 however, the price of lead fell and many mines had to close.

Edward I had admired many castles that he had seen in France and wanted one at Fflint fashioned on that of Tour-de-Constance at Aigues Montes in Provence. Edward arrived at Fflint with his engineer, Richard L'Engenour, in 1277, having crossed the Dee from the Wirral. With him he had an army 1,130 'volunteers', including woodsmen, dykers and ditchers 340 skilled craftsmen. There was also an armed escort. The forest was cleared and on July 25, 1277 work began on Fflint Castle. Nothing was spared and £1,000 was spent on its construction by the end of 1277.

Considerable amounts of sandstone were brought from the Wirral and Edward also began to build a small town with extensive defences.

Owain Glyndŵr and Hywel Gwynedd, a close relative, attacked Fflint Castle on different occasions, both of them unsuccessfully. Hywel was spectacularly unsuccessful because he was caught and lost his head for his troubles. Henry V controlled Fflint during the reign of Glyndŵr, pardoning the County of Fflint for a payment of 500 marks. On the death of Henry V the castle was given to his widow whom later married Owain Tudur, the founder of the House of Tudor. The castle played no part in the War of the Roses (1455-1485) and little is known of it until the Civil War of 1642-1648.

Charles I enjoyed the support of most of the controlling families of north Wales and very little trouble was experienced in raising cash or support for an army from the county of Fflint. Colonel Roger Mostyn, then just 22 years of age, quickly raised his own private army of over one thousand supporters from Flintshire alone and, at his own expense, ordered that Fflint castle should be restored to its former strength as its military significance was obvious in any forthcoming war. Mostyn had charge over Hawarden, Fflint and Mostyn castles to defend the north-eastern Welsh coast and the main route into north Wales from the midlands, Cheshire or Shropshire.

Through trickery or a badly worded message, Sir Thomas Myddleton of Chirk Castle and Sir William Brereton seized Hawarden castle during 1643. Flushed with success Myddleton moved onto Fflint Castle and put it under siege. After the occupants had eaten all the horses, dogs and any other source of food they could find, they were forced to surrender under the condition that each man would return to his own home without arms and never raise them again.

On December 22 1646 Parliament ordered that Fflint castle be destroyed. Cannon fire was used and miners dug under the foundations so as to build a fire under the stones. The heat from the fire caused the stone to crack and collapse, fetching a section of wall down with it. Although the Civil War itself raged on until 1648, Fflint became a quiet and subdued part of the county. Many tradesmen left to seek business elsewhere and much of the town fell into decay.

Forty-six of Mostyn's men had escaped from Fflint castle and Mostyn was not about to give in. He set sail for Ireland where he raised another army, this time of Irish supporters, who returned with him to Mostyn docks. The two thousand Irish Rangers were so ill from the journey that many vowed that, should they survive the war, they would never return to their native soil for fear of the journey by sea.

*An aerial photograph of the Roman fort at Caer Gai, Llanuwchllyn.*

*Llyn Tegid (Bala Lake) from the air.*

*Canoeing on Afon Tryweryn.*

*The Dee bridge at Corwen.*

*Stone arches crossing the river at Carrog.*

*Llangar church, Corwen.*

*Berwyn Station, Llangollen.*

*Eliseg pillar, near Glyn y Groes, Llangollen.*

*Horseshoe falls, Llangollen.*

*The river Dee in flood, Llangollen.*

*The canal museum at Llangollen.*

*Railway pool, Llangollen.*

*The Telford viaduct for the Llangollen canal at Pontcysyllte.*

*Llanasa church.*

*Erbistock weir.*

*Holt castle.*

*Ewloe castle.*

*King Charles Tower, Chester city walls.*

*Grosvenor bridge, Chester.*

*W.E. Gladstone opening Queensferry bridge, 1897.*

*Ruin of Basingwerk Abbey, Greenfield.*

*Flint castle.*

*Connah's Quay dock.*

76

*Two of the last ships at the British Steel jetty, Connah's Quay.*

*Unloading at Mostyn Dock.*

77

*Mostyn Dock.*

*Lorries testing new Queensferry Bridge, 1926.*

*Bob Manifold*                    *Joe Fellows*

*Foryd harbour.*

*Point of Air lighthouse.*

Colonel Mostyn paid for being on the losing side. He had spent a vast amount on his cause, and Parliament took a further one tenth of his better estate. His wife also died suddenly at this time, leaving him a broken man. However his despair and financially challenged state did not last long for he was richly rewarded on the restoration of the monarchy.

Fflint Castle is now under the control of CADW. The property is open all the year round and there are ample parking facilities. The importance of the siting of this castle is obvious at low water, when the track is apparent across the estuary to Shotwick.

Fflint town slowly recovered after the Civil War. The small but attractive 13th century church was badly damaged by Sir William Brereton whose men ripped out the carved woodwork and masonry, and took the metal from the organ pipes. The little church was left to deteriorate and by the mid-19th century a bell had been erected at a hall in the town centre so that the faithful may be called to worship. The decision was taken in 1848 to demolish the church and rebuild it. The new church had a bell-tower donated by P Ellis-Eyton the MP for Flintshire.

Fflint had a reputation for the cruellest gaols in the country. The first gaol was built somewhere in Church Street and men and women were kept in chains in the one dark damp room with little light, food or water. Conditions were so bad that many people took their own lives rather than serve out their sentence. A gallows had been erected in the town centre but they were unable to find a local executioner. Men came from as far away as Shropshire and Derbyshire to carry out the grim task.

The 'House of Correction' in Church Street remained open until 1785 when it was forced to close after mounting public disquiet at the conditions. The new gaol was built within what was left of Fflint Castle and it was widely advertised as being humane, the elders of Fflint doubtless anxious to erase the terrible name of the gaol in Church Street. Conditions were indeed a vast improvement on the old one, with better facilities and a regular visit from the priest. The people however were far from happy with the newfangled gaol and following public disquiet it was closed in 1870, the prisoners being transferred to Mold. The people of Fflint then had a small problem of walking sixteen miles to see loved ones.

Among the last prisoners to serve time at Fflint Castle would have been colliers from Mold. They would have been the leaders of the Mold Riots of 1869, when colliers rebelled against their English landlords, removing them from the county by force on horse and cart. The leaders were charged with common assault and sentenced to severe terms of imprisonment at Fflint Castle. Whether the rioters from Mold were returned to the new gaol at Mold is not recorded.

Henry VIII appointed a Court of Assize in Fflint and another at Caerwys. If a judge from outside Flintshire were appointed to sit, he was to be met at the county boundary by the High Sheriff for the county and escorted to a local safe house, which he used for the duration of the case. This practise continued until the Assize Courts were replaced by the Crown Courts, which sit almost continually making escorts totally impractical. The judge then had quarters within the courts themselves and a local police escort. Mold had become the sole Assize Court for the county of Fflint and the Crown Court is also situated there.

By the turn of the 18th century Fflint was no place to be caught doing wrong, with public floggings being commonplace for men and women. The unfortunate were ordered by the court to be stripped to the waist and flogged 'until there was blood on them'. Victims had to walk the main street so as to be flogged before onlookers, often for offences such as begging or being without a place of abode. The practise came to an end in 1817 because of public pressure, including violent marches by Fflint residents. Public hangings continued until 1868 when pressure also brought this barbaric practise to an end. Fflint courts also sentenced people, often for very minor violations of the law, to serve a term of deportation in the colonies of the British Empire. But rioting against authority was still commonplace in Fflint throughout the 18th and 19th centuries.

Concern about public order had grown to such an extent by 1834 that a local man was sworn in as constable, charged with keeping the town peaceful. Problems arose because of rioting colliers from Lancashire and Cheshire who came seeking work on the Welsh coastal mining strip. There was also a large Irish population in the ports of the area. A list of alehouses showed that there were thirty-five in Flint alone in the 1840's. The situation continued to deteriorate so that the Flint corporation appointed another local man as sergeant of the police in 1857. He was supplied with a horse, saddle and stables plus a weekly wage of 23/- per week. This was a fair sum, being more than the colliers received for two weeks work.

Cholera hit the town in 1832 and again in 1849. Riots ensued, as usual, because 'strangers to the town of Flint' were blamed. In the attack of 1849 the brother of Charles Kingsley (the poet and author of 'The Sands of Dee') was staying with friends at nearby Kelsterton and came to assist the sick and dying. Kingsley himself came and stayed with the same Kelsterton family and it is said that, whilst there, he wrote his famous poem.

Fflint was a busy port town, handling 8,429 tons of cargo in 1905. The main trade was in coal and lead from local mines, and also chemicals from local factories. The port was incorporated into the Courtauld's Castle Complex when that company established in the town. The Castle Works have since been demolished and the area is now the site of an industrial complex with a new road system to the small factory units. The dock itself is badly silted, but part of the original wooden supporting wall remains, as do the sluices. The flushing pool was filled in long ago. The dock now has several small fishing boats and discarded older boats. It is very scenic but hasn't any industrial use today.

Fflint played its part in the tale of the *Royal Charter*. She was grounded just off Fflint after her launch, receiving considerable damage to her bottom plates. She was towed from here to Liverpool for repair and later. She left there for Australia but sank on her return journey with the loss of four hundred and thirty-four lives and quite a bit of gold.

With the coming of the railway, Fflint took on a new role as a seaside resort, many flocking here to bathe and holiday in summer. Claims were made that the waters at Fflint had miracle healing powers and many sick people came to take them. Subsequent tests found nothing to support the claim, but the tourist trade loved it and did well. New industry also came with the Courtauld's factories all along the estuary and the subsequent demand for housing caused an expansion of the villages along the coast.

Adjacent to the castle remains is the modern lifeboat station, which is of immense importance to the estuary, having a long history of saving lives.

We have to imagine the foreshore during the Middle Ages because there have been massive changes here recently and big gutters have appeared and disappeared as the sands and silts increased. Probably most of what is now green would have been soft sands before the river was canalized. We know from the writings of Edward I that there were considerable forests from Fflint towards the west, and that the trees extended onto the foreshore. Evidence of this can be seen at Chester Record Office where a 1910 photograph clearly shows tree roots at low water on the foreshore near Neston. Some of the old sketches of Fflint Castle show ships actually tied to the castle walls and were probably quite accurate, although today only the highest of tides come in that close.

Today, all of the Dee estuary is governed by various Acts of Parliament, controlling the bass breeding area, the salmon and sea-trout netting operations etc. It is amazing how the pleas of the fishermen of the estuary were ignored when the industrial giants of the Fflint area were polluting the estuary – a problem that they, of course, claimed did not exist. As with many environmental issues, the 'scaremongers' were proven correct for, when the industries went and the chemical discharges stopped, fish and especially shellfish returned in huge numbers. Pollution, what pollution?

The last word about Fflint is its fascinating dialect. They have a curious way of talking in English and in Welsh, due maybe to Fflint's connections with the sea. One quirk is their answer to the question: 'Where do you come from?' Their answer, especially the older natives, is always: 'Off Flint'. Discussing this curious matter with a colleague once led him to the remark 'I've never known a place where so many people were born in boats – out at sea'.

# Bagillt

In the 17th and 18th centuries Bagillt was a very busy port, moving over 1,000 tons of locally cut coal a week when the local collieries were at their height.

As with many other small ports, there was some difficulty in reaching the deeper channel out in the estuary and, in the days of sail, ships could be held in port for days waiting for the winds to ease. Their departure then depended on the tide and its height. There is no wonder that the railway was so successful here.

But before the railway came, the only way to move heavy materials like stone, coal and ore to a rapidly expanding world was directly by sea from here. These ports were ideally situated so that money making mine owners could export from nearby Halkyn with its valuable seams of minerals that had been mined since Roman times.

Crossing the Dee at this point prior to canalization was only possible on foot, or by a very limited ferry service that was only available to horse-drawn carriages.

Bagillt port is now silted up although part of the wooden supports that once formed a part of the dockside remain. There has been considerable erosion here and locals claim that as much as a quarter of a mile of land has disappeared, much of it good grazing land that has been reclaimed by the sea. There is also a landfill site close to the edge of the marsh and it is very difficult to see how wide or how long the dock actually was with the extensive erosion that has occurred here, especially in recent years.

The landfill site is where a copper-works once stood and it is adjacent to what used to be a colliery. Also adjacent to the old colliery, there were huge spoil-tips that have been levelled. They have also been used to fill part of the port and one of the flushing-pools, known as 'Reservoir 773'. There is one flushing-pool visible off the A548 on the left when travelling from Bagillt to Fflint, this being part of the second Bagillt port, known as 'Dee Banks Gutter'. It has been claimed that Samuel Pepys sailed from 'Dee Banks Gutter' when he stayed in the area. Most of the passenger trade went from here, whilst the Bagillt dock handled the cargo trade.

The main Bagillt dock still retains much of its presence thanks to a considerable flow of water through the still intact sluice-gates, The water originates from the mines above Halkyn. The flow helps because it flushes any sludge brought in by the tide. As can be seen on most of this coastline the NRA has carried out extensive work with huge boulders to prevent further erosion from rising sea levels. The port is a haven for small fishing boats.

Access to both docks is from the A548 at Bagillt. It is worth a visit on a clear day if only for the views across the estuary and to see the tide rising. There is excellent fishing hereabouts in summer and winter, with cod and bass coming close in.

There was at one time a passenger ferry service from Bagillt to Parkgate, from where a traveller could obtain a fast stagecoach to Liverpool. But in strong winds the ships were unable to get away from Bagillt, meaning that the connections at Liverpool were missed, and the service was lost for ever. The problem was caused by the unpredictable weather off Hilbre Island. Attempts were made to form a trade between Bagillt and Ireland but this was again ruined by the weather. The ferry was withdrawn and later used at Runcorn. In 1821 the very first steamship *Cambria* made trips from Hoylake to Bagillt taking just over one hour. This service lasted until 1825. The ferry from Bagillt had been abandoned by 1840 as the railway took much trade and the unpredictable estuary weather took its toll on ships and men.

# Greenfield

The Greenfield valley runs from Holywell town to the coast at what was Greenfield dock. The area first came to prominence long before the Norman Conquest, when the legend of St Winifreds' well became famous. Such was the impact of the story that it became the Welsh equivalent of Lourdes, drawing pilgrims from afar.

Winifred (Gwenfrewi) was born of noble blood in the 7th century and, when a young lady, was raped and beheaded by a suitor, Prince Caradog of Penarlâg, for refusing his advances. Her uncle Beuno who was, thankfully, a saint, witnessed Caradogs folly and proceeded to reattach Gwenfrewi/Winifred's head to her body, and then revived her. From the spot where her blood fell, a well sprang. Winifred went on a pilgrimage to Rome before returning to live with saint Eleri in Gwytherin, near Llanrwst, where she died. Her remains were moved to Shrewsbury Abbey in 1137.

The spring was said to have healing properties and became a shrine to St Winifred. Amazing claims have been made ever since of people and animals being cured by drinking or bathing in the waters of the well. As with many of these wells, there is no explaining the phenomenon since scientists have analysed the water, showing that there is clearer and cleaner water from springs close by. There is nothing out of the ordinary about the water of this particular well. But the claims continue to be made.

By the 11th century there was a church and a castle nearby giving the many pilgrims to the site a centre that they could use before Basingwerk Abbey was founded in 1131/32 by Ranulf II, Earl of Chester.

Basingwerk Abbey was founded for the Order of Savigny but was taken over by the Cistercians in 1147. An important function of the abbey was to look after visitors to St Winifreds Well. In the records of Henry II it is described as being 'a chapel of Basingwerk wherein people dwelt'. When Geraldus Cambrensis travelled through Greenfield in 1188, he described the area as having a few occupied houses.

Richard, Earl of Chester was one of the pilgrims who paid homage to the Well of St Winifred, but was caught in a trap when he stayed at the abbey. Assuming that a nasty situation was about to arise, he sent a messenger to Chester requiring William Fitz-Nigel, the Constable of the day, to fetch 'a great army with all haste'.

The Constable arranged this and went via the Wirral to Hilbre, seeking boats to cross the Dee. None were to be had and the Monk at Hilbre Island suggested that they pray to St Winifred for help. Apparently their prayers were answered because the Dee parted in the manner of the Red Sea, allowing Moses the Constable and his army to cross safely to the Welsh side of the estuary, where they saved the Earl's bacon.

Everyone was grateful and Hilbre Island and 'all the lands between Hilbre and Basingwerk Abbey' were bestowed upon the monks of Basingwerk. This is an explanation that is given for the areas called 'the Constable banks' in the estuary.

During the 13th century the abbey was protected by the House of Gwynedd and Edward I, the latter issuing a letter of protection stating that on no account should the monks have anything to do with local people or with the enemies of the King. Edward I stayed at Basingwerk Abbey in 1277, from where he laid plans for his assaults on north Wales. He was also able to oversee the building of Fflint castle and police the crossing from Fflint to Shotwick across the estuary.

Tomos ap Dafydd Pennant was the abbot at the monastery until he had to resign because he had a desire to marry. His son Nicholas who turned out to be the last abbot in 1536, when the property was granted to the Crown because of the Dissolution succeeded him. Its gross income at that time was £163.7.11d and Nicholas received a pension of £17 per annum. Following Dissolution, the building was dismantled.

Lead from the abbey was used to restore Holt Castle and other useable parts went to Dublin Castle in 1546. Some of the roof went to build Cilcain Parish Church and some of the stained glass went to Llanasa Church.

Henry ap Harry of Llanasa and Peter Mutton of Meliden took control of the site in 1540. Following the marriage of Henry ap Harry's daughter to one of the Mostyns of Talacre, it came under the control of the Mostyn family. The Mostyns made part of the Abbey habitable and it was lived in until the 18th century. Miss Clementina Mostyn placed the ruins in the hands of the State in 1923. It is now looked after by CADW.

But despite the Dissolution of the Monasteries and the violent prejudice against Roman Catholics, people continued to travel to Holywell and business flourished. By the end of the 17th century Holywell was the largest town in north-eastern Wales, and water from the holy well was by then providing power to fulling mills, malting kilns and a limekiln in the valley, and there was a direct route to the Greenfield docks.

In 1590 one Samuel Flete built a lead smelting works using charcoal, which caused so much pollution to both air and water that local people turned on him and pulled his factory down. A Madam Kaye made another attempt to smelt lead in 1733, on land owned by Roger Pennant of Downing, Whitford. Pollution was again a problem and lawsuits flew until the factory closed.

The Mostyn estate books show that in 1728 they received rent for an iron-forge, three wire mills and a red-lead mill. There was also a corn-mill. The ponds visible today were mostly dug in the 18th century to provide a source of power to the different mills in the valley, and were enlarged as was needed. The water from St Winifred's Well produced a flow-rate of four thousand gallons a minute at a temperature of 46°F, which meant no frost trouble: the steepness of the valley gave a good flow, thus giving much power. The first cotton spinning mills went up in 1777 powered by water and new and larger six-storey buildings were erected: Upper Mill (1783), Lower Mill (1785) and Crescent Mill (1790), all powered by water

By 1780 much of the site of the present Grosvenor Chater Mills was under the control of the Parys Mine Company of Anglesey, from where copper ingots were sent to Greenfield for smelting. A major discovery in 1783 was the process of making strong bolts from copper. Experiments had been ongoing for many decades to prevent teredo worms from attacking ships' hulls in tropical waters. Lining the hull with copper worked, but the copper corroded the iron bolts that held the copper sheetto the hull. Thomas Williams of the Parys Mine was able to produce copper bolts that were strong enough to be a good substitute for the iron ones. Patents ensured that the work could only be done at the Greenfield works, and so the Greenfield Copper & Brass Company was born in association with John Wilkinson, the ironmaster from the Bersham foundry near Wrexham. The fame of the product attracted worldwide trade.

Lead had been mined in the Holywell and Halkyn area at least since Roman times. In 1773 the first known leases for the Holywell Level Lead Mines came into being, the whole site being surveyed by June 1774, but it seems that profits were scarce until 1796. The entrance level also drained the mine and became something of a tourist attraction by 1778, with trips by boat along the level, and picnic tables being placed in one of the caverns. By about 1830 however, the boats had been replaced by a tramway.

By the 1880's Holywell was the biggest town in the County of Fflint with over five and a half thousand people recorded as living there. There was by this time a continuous line of factories from the well of St Winifred down to the docks at Greenfield, with rows of houses built especially to accommodate the workers. It was a prosperous place indeed. Thomas Pennant wrote that there were twelve hundred and twenty-five employed in the cotton industry, including men, women, children and apprentices, with another two hundred in the surrounding parishes also supplying aids to the mills. He also spoke highly of the sleeping accommodation for the workers, Pennant recorded less employment in the copper and brass foundaries, with ninety-three in the copper forge, and fifty each in the brass foundry and rolling mills.

The American and Napoleonic wars put copper in decline, and the end was also in sight for high-grade ore from Mynydd Parys in Anglesey (Ynys Môn). Changes occurred constantly in the Dee channel and ships found difficulty in getting in and out of the docks. By the 1820's the heady days of Holywell copper were gone; by 1872 the Greenfield lead-works had been demolished, and the Holywell Copper firm finally closed-down in 1894.

It is possible that the cotton mills had installed a steam engine by 1790, and only employed seven hundred and thirty-six people by 1816, twenty of these under the age of 10. The company struggled through wilful arson, severe flooding and other difficulties such as the markets for spun-cotton being in Lancashire and so far away. Holywell was also at a serious disadvantage because of a lack of weaving skills. In addition the owners invested in the lead-mines, which then went into serious decline. Finally, when the Douglas & Smalley bank at Mold collapsed, the company went into liquidation and the industries that had long brought prosperity to Holywell and the area faded away. By 1906, unable to discover any new veins, the Holywell Level mine also went into liquidation and closed.

Some new industries took over the old mills but most were short lived and came to nothing. An exception was the Welsh Flannel Manufacturing Company, formed in 1874 to work at the lower and upper mills. The joint-owners were William Brown (of Browns of Chester) and Urias Bromley, this being a measure to counter the high unemployment in Holywell since the older mills closed. Two hundred jobs were provided. Thomas Waterhouse took over the firm in 1902 and, despite fires and major floods, it survived, the Waterhouse family relinquishing their interests only in 1957. By the 1980's it was producing fine woollen goods mostly from Jacob's Sheep fleeces.

In addition to the cotton, lead and copper industries, there were lesser industries of stone-crushing, battery making, woollen mills and coalmines that were too small to make any real impact. The railways came in the late 1860s, but that did not help. The three-foot gauge horse drawn railway from the lead mines to the dock and a line into Holywell were failures partly because, as ships grew, so the need for deeper ports than Holywell and Greenfield became apparent. A gradient of 1:27 also made the Holywell line the steepest passenger line in Britain. Trade slowly died away as traders sought to use better and faster facilities elsewhere. The narrow-gauge lines were finally connected to the main Chester – Holyhead line.

Throughout history the main draw to the area, and its main source of wealth, has been the spring water from St Winifred's well. A building was erected over the well in 1490. But persecution of Roman Catholics affected the area following the Dissolution. In 1636-37 an order was made by the anti Roman Catholic Government to close all inns, remove railings, report all visitors to the Magistrate, and to disfigure any statutes in the area of the well. On James II's succession in 1686, repairs were made and restoration carried out. Further persecution in the 18th century caused more damage and in 1723 the building was turned into a school. But despite the attacks and persecution, pilgrims still came here from all over Britain.

In 1821-2 after a severe winter, there was serious flooding mostly due to increased flow from feeder streams. In April 1859 the mills temporarily lost their water supply when part of the stream had to be diverted and the basin drained to repair the shrine and the chapel. No other case of interrupted flow was recorded until 1917 when the Milwr tunnel was cut to drain water from the Halkyn lead-mines. Once tapped, the spring dried up. It was restored but the flow was considerably less than in the pre 1917 days. Until 1926 the reservoirs below the mills were used to supply the area with water, a blind water-carrier selling water at ¾d per bucket.

In 1780's a flushing-pool was made at the rear of Greenfield dock to help flush the silts and to increase space for ships to berth. Sheds and warehouses were built alongside and rented out to individual firms for storage. During the 18th century especially, Greenfield docks traded extensively with Liverpool and foreign parts. In 1802 a sail-ship ferry was in force between Greenfield and Parkgate and also Chester. It later moved to Bagillt because more money could be made from carrying cargo than people from Greenfield.

An iron steamer called *Fanny* was in use in 1857 plying between Greenfield and Liverpool, the fare being 5/-d in a cabin and 4/-d on deck. It was a busy ship with pilgrims to St Winifred's from Lancashire, and the service continued until the mid-1860s when it was replaced by the Lord Mostyn coach service. Neither could compete with the railways, however. In 1870 a fresh ferry attempt was made with the *St Winifred* and in 1879, the *Shamrock*, but both failed in under a year. The *St Winifred* was a paddle steamer, built for the Holywell & Liverpool Packet Company. It was one hundred and thirty feet long, carrying forty tons of cargo and three hundred passengers. By 1890 Newton Keates had leased almost seven hundred feet of the wharf but, when this firm closed, the remaining users felt that maintaining the wharf was not justifiable, sending it into serious decline.

The dock was once a considerable place, capable of berthing fair sized ships such as the *St Winifred*. Today it is silted up; the flushing-pool is grassed over and the dock is full of rotting fishing boats, most of them small rowing or outboard engine boats. The wooden quayside has long gone for firewood. Much damage was caused by the National Rivers Authority's anti-flooding scheme, with large boulders and concrete blocks being tipped to form a wall so as to keep the water from the sewage and gas works just a few yards inland. It is a pity that such an important link with the Greenfield Valley should be allowed to decay in such a way but, perhaps one day, its potential as an historical port will be appreciated. This has already happened to the old mills and the abbey ruins.

The people of Holywell and Greenfield have long been known for their forthrightness - they call a spade a spade. There is though a tale from July 23rd 1684, when the Duke of Beaufort came to stay with Sir Roger Mostyn, so as to view the militia at nearby Rhosesmor. They avoided Holywell as much as possible, with the exception of St Winifred's Well, because 'at Holly Well the inhabitants they speake Welsh, and go barefoot and bare leg'd. They are a nasty sort of people'. The inhabitants' opinion of Mostyn and his cronies were not recorded or, if they were, they would probably not be printable.

## Llanerch-y-Môr

This is a small private dock that was used in connection with the coal-trade from local privately owned collieries. According to the *Ports Book* of 1905 it handled 847 tons of cargo in that year.

Today, this small port is the home of an ex-British Rail Isle of Man ferryboat that somebody once called a 'fun-ship'. It has been used as a market, an entertainment theatre, a gambling house and goodness knows what else. It is a landmark in the area, but bitterly opposed by locals. The ship is set in concrete and unlikely to move ever again.

Close-by is the business that is widely known as *Abacan*, although many people erroneously think its name is *Abercan*.

## Mostyn Docks

This is now the only active port left on the Dee estuary. The dock recently had permission to extend docking facilities so as to take the roll-on / roll-off ferries for Ireland as well as bigger cargo ships. Current trade is in scrap-metal to Spain, wood pulp and cut timber from Sweden, the export of fertiliser, and also rolled-steel from the Shotton steel mills. The dock's customs and excise office has been there since the days of the English Civil War. It also has its own flushing-pool to keep the dock basin clean.

Strikes and industrial disputes on Merseyside in the 1970's saw much trade diverted to smaller ports like Mostyn. Ironically, after the problems were resolved bigger and faster ships came on the scene and the smaller ports missed out. Rejuvenating the Birkenhead docks did much damage to Mostyn Docks and Summers Wharf, hence the need for Mostyn to have a new and bigger dock. Mostyn does not suffer from silting, but it is limited to ships of 4000 tons.

Exactly when the port was first built is uncertain, but it was operational during the English Civil War in the 17th century, and may have been built over one hundred years earlier. It is said that Jasper Tudor, uncle to Henry VII, escaped from here in 1471, having climbed through a broken window at Mostyn Hall. He apparently laid an amount of straw across his back, disguising himself sufficiently to fool Richard III's searching troops. He then sailed from Mostyn docks for France, but landed in Brittany and stayed there for thirteen years.

During the reign of William III this part of the north Wales coast was rife with the smuggling of tobacco, wines and French linen. The local gentry were deeply involved and there was a never-ending battle against the Customs men. Thomas Pennant records that, in 1702, a raid in Mostyn recovered sixty pipes of French wine from a nearby barn. It was taken to the local inn, The Honest Man, for safekeeping overnight but, during the night, so called *coal miners* raided the inn, the customs men were tied-up and the wine was taken.

Despite claims that it was colliers who took the wine, the customs men hotly denied this. According to them, colliers did not wear lace collars and cuffs, with jewellery around their necks – they claimed that it was the gentry. Nobody discovered who raided the pub but the landlord never went short of anything for the rest of his life. With most of the north Wales coast from Fflint to Llandudno in the hands of one family, it was most unwise to have an opinion as to who did what in the smuggling game. With the Mostyns being the landowners and main employers, it was extremely difficult surviving without them. The customs men left the area in a sorry state, commenting that it was nigh impossible to police that part of north Wales.

The inn mentioned in the raid is of great interest. It is still known as The Honest Man and has the date 1699 etched over the doorway. Its exact date is uncertain, as is the identity of its builder. It has been suggested that it was here before the Civil War, but the date above the door is fifty years later making this unlikely. Pennant thought it might have been a man from Gloucestershire who thought it was an ideal location for an inn; others think it may have been the Mostyn estate as they owned the land. Over the door there is a figure of a man's head and a sheep. A story says that a local man stole a sheep but suffered pangs of guilt before killing it and returned it to its owner, alive and well. Stealing a sheep in those days was a hanging offence, but this man was classed as honest thereafter.

Another story is that one of the first licensees was a man who, without fail, discharged all of his debts; he always bought with cash and so became known as the honest man. Mostyn Estates Office sold the inn to Burtonwood Breweries in 1913.

The place certainly has character, including a ghost. The present licensee has tales of a male dressed in the outfit of a Cavalier similar to those of the Civil War period, complete with thigh boots. There is also said to be an old man dressed in clothes of perhaps the 17th or 18th century, and who sits in a chair staring into what was the fireplace, or smiling at onlookers. The storage of wineglasses and other items was altered when they were sent flying across the pub late at night by an unseen force. The ghost is still described as being 'friendly'.

Further intrigue is added to the story of the inn by the underground tunnel that runs from its lounge to the old part of Mostyn dock, and another tunnel that runs to the Mostyn estate. The tunnels were of course the highways of the smugglers but are now in a state of collapse and have been boarded up. The colliers were probably responsible for these, even if they only had a very small share of the smuggled goods from their noble superiors.

Although modernised and reinforced with concrete, the dock known today as *Number 3* is thought to be the original dock. Until fairly recently made of wood, it was here that Colonel Mostyn landed his Irish volunteers in 1643. Guns and ammunitions were also smuggled through Mostyn during the Civil War. The port also played a role during the reign of William of Orange and during the Napoleonic wars.

Human cargo also came through Mostyn during the late 17th century in the form of females who were brought from Ireland to supply a certain service. From the small ports around Wales, they expanded to run the oldest business known to man in the bigger cities of England. The gentry reigned supreme in the area, goods of all kinds coming and going more or less freely since the customs had no semblance of a control.

Moses Griffith, illustrator of Thomas Pennant's book *A History of*

*Whitford and Mostyn* sketched The Honest Man on an area of flat ground surrounded by high rocks, with the Dee lapping the frontage of the inn. How much of this is artist's licence is uncertain, but it was said that ships were then tied to trees on the shoreline near the inn.

The manor of Mostyn for much of its history has remained under the control of the Lordship of Mostyn. The title Mostyn was first taken by Piers, the third son of Richard ap Hywel of Mostyn, in 1542, having received land from his father under a deed dated 11th April 1522. Mostyn Hall is not open to the public but private visits can be arranged by writing to the present Lord Mostyn. It was a vast estate in its time, covering twenty-five thousand acres of Flintshire and some two thousand acres in Gwynedd. There was also land in other parts of the country. Probably built on wealth from mining operations in the Clwydian Range, it is still a considerable estate today covering land from Talacre to beyond Llandudno, including land on which the town of Llandudno itself is built. This was partly acquired through enclosure acts in 1841, when the then Lord Mostyn was the Member of Parliament for the area. Common land would become the property of the MP through an Act of Parliament, the MP receiving an area of land in direct proportion to the amount they already owned; thence the more land one already owned, then the more land one was entitled to claim under enclosure acts.

Much has already been written of the involvement of Colonel Sir Roger Mostyn in the English Civil War, and his subsequent punishment. The Mostyn family has certainly not been without its problems and there were severe squabbles over land, money and marriage. Sir Piers Mostyn, seems to have been a little of a black sheep, marrying a Catholic and thus splitting the family ranks. He went on to build Talacre Hall and began acquiring vast amounts of land. It was he who took advantage of the Dissolution of the Monasteries, acquiring Basingwerk Abbey and its land.

There have been three Talacre Halls. The first dates from the time of Piers Mostyn in the mid 16th century, and was enlarged in 1750. The building was entirely rebuilt in 1824 but this one was destroyed by fire in 1827. The present building was erected in 1829. In its day as a Hall it is said to have housed vast numbers of original oil masterpieces by Gainsborough and other eminent painters.

By 1919 serious money was needed to pay death duties and Talacre Hall was sold to nuns of the Benedictine Order. They acquired a wonderful reputation for making homemade sweets and jams, which they sold in their shop on the premises. The nuns went under the name of 'Our Lady Help of Christians'. They also made the robes for the monks of the Benedictine Order at nearby Pantasaph and other places within the UK.

Throughout the life of Talacre Hall it has had a tall tower which countless sailors have used as a landmark from the estuary. Today in summer the foliage is such that the tower is now hardly visible. Another nearby property was Tan Llan Hall, also at one time occupied by the Mostyns. It is now a caravan site and little is known of the place.

It was the Mostyn family who drained the vast areas of marshlands in the Talacre area by planting scrub and burying trees and other matter to prevent erosion from the incoming tides. Most of this reclaimed land is now either farmland or under caravans. The Chester to Holyhead railway also runs over it. The main A548 roadway was until fairly recent times impassable on a single mule and totally unsuitable for a carriage. The erosion of the coastline is today worse than ever due they say to rising seas. Once again workmen can be seen from Talacre to Connah's Quay repairing and reinforcing the embankment with huge stones so as to keep the sea from reclaiming what was rightfully hers in the first place.

Coal has been mined in the Mostyn area since 1284 and maybe earlier. There was a time when there were two small pits situated actually on the quayside and the coal was transferred to a waiting ship. A lot went to Ireland but there was also trade with Anglesey.

In World War II the of coast from Mostyn to Rhyl and beyond was heavily fortified. Apart from anti-tank ditches, there were also pill-boxes and one still stands at the end of the quay on Mostyn dock. Out at sea, model planes were towed for the artillery to practise firing and there are many accounts of dogfights between British and German aircraft over the Talacre and Mostyn coastal area. Much of the reclaimed land also served as firing ranges for mortars and rifle-fire as the troops and home guard went through their drills.

Close to Mostyn docks was the Darwen & Mostyn Ironworks. It was always exciting to pass it on the main railway line as the furnaces were being tapped and there was a huge glow as smoke and steam surged out of the place. It had a raillink to the main railway line and it went through the works onto Mostyn docks, where much of the raw material was imported. It was built in the early 19th century and had little problems as its raw materials were all close at hand and its finished products could be exported off the doorstep. The works became known as The Darwen & Mostyn Iron Company in 1887. The coming of the mainline railway caused the premises to be expanded and it specialized in producing ferro-manganese. The works closed in 1964 and was dismantled. It is now part of the dock complex, although its engine sheds are still there to see.

The first steamship to operate from Mostyn was *Cambria*. She had a run to Liverpool and called at Bagillt to collect fare-paying passengers.

This started in 1821 but did not last long. November 11, 1829 saw the *Hercules*, which was also a steamer, tie-up at Mostyn Dock. She sailed to Liverpool docks, and later had a passenger trade between Foryd (Rhyl), Bagillt and Liverpool. This service lasted just four years.

The *Liverpool Daily Post* reported on 5.8.1967 that Mostyn Docks planned to increase its annual tonnage from 100,000 tons to 400,000 tons. They had received 166 ships during the year, which was double the 1966 number, and the dock manager complained that too many ships left the dock with ballast.

A report of October 26 1968 in the same newspaper proposed that there was to be a new weekly service to and from Belfast, and they hoped to increase this to three or four times a week. Sadly this never came to anything.

In 1994 a German registered freighter *UNITAS H* docked at Mostyn loaded with wood pulp, having come from Estonia in the Baltic. Her cargo was bound for the Kronospan factory at Chirk. One of the crew was sent for a brush to clean the hatches but was overcome by fumes in the hold and died instantly. The chief officer, on realising that something was wrong, followed him and met with the same fate. Sadly, neither wore the breathing apparatus that is supplied to prevent such accidents, where toxic gases escape from the wood cargo.

Much of the wood imported into Mostyn is bound for either Chirk or the Shotton Paper Company, which has a massive plant on the reclaimed land at Shotton's new industrial estate. Since 1992 Mostyn docks has also had the contract to load and unload the ships at British Steel Wharf on the monthly high tides.

The policing and buoy maintenance of the estuary now rests with the Environmental Authority – late The National Rivers Authority. They took it over from Trinity House in May 1995. The EA is now responsible for marking out the channel and lighting the buoys and perches. They have their own building on the end of Mostyn dock by the old World War II pillbox.

# Llanasa

The delightful village of Llanasa is just a couple of miles off the A548 coast road and is clearly marked. Central to the village is the attractive church. Llanasa was first mentioned in the Domesday Book of 1086 and is dedicated to St Asaph. It is claimed that there was a place of worship in

Llanasa on the site of the present church as far back as the 7th century. Sir Piers Mostyn of Talacre Hall sent many of the dead who were washed-up on the foreshore at Talacre to Llanasa for burial. It is unclear whether this was actually in Llanasa Church, or within the parish of Llanasa. Near to the site of Talacre Abbey (Hall) there is a steep wooded slope covered in conifer trees. Some forty or fifty years ago it is said that there were gravestones here, but that these were removed and trees planted. Enquiries with the Sister Abbess who was at Talacre Abbey until it closed were negative; she being sure that no records of a graveyard exist. But others are quite adamant that this would be the area where Sir Piers buried the dead of any tragedy on the river.

The beautiful church is worth a visit. The font is 14th century and obviously hand-carved. The windows at the eastern and western ends are of particular interest as it is said that they came from Basingwerk Abbey following the Dissolution of the Monasteries. The chalice and pattern used in Holy Communion are both hand-carved and of solid silver with a sheep's head hall-mark.

The parish records of 1855-1860 show that the parish then contained 6,000 acres and this was divided into townships. In 1855 there were some 2,732 people there. The graveyard was enlarged in 1844, and again in 1860.

The vicarage was enlarged in 1856 at a cost of £245.11.6d. The extension consisted of home, office, dove-cote, barn, stable and cow-house, all covered in thatch including the pigsty. The brew-house was also re-roofed at a cost of £2.16.6d. Hostilities broke out on August 6, 1860 because of a plan to build a Roman Catholic school in Llanasa before constructing a Church of England School. The Lords of the Manor (the Mostyn's) were Catholic at that time.

The Vicar of Llanasa wrote to the Bishop in a state of fury pointing out that £600-£700 had been given for the erection of this school and yet, from a total of over two thousand parishioners, less than one hundred were Roman Catholics. The grant however did not arrive until 1868.

Llanasa like most Welsh villages has haunting tales. One such is of an old mariner who can be seen on the road to Llanasa, searching for lost shipmates who were taken from him in a wreck one stormy night.

Another, probably true, story goes back to the 17th century when William Griffith, a sailor, stumbled into the village alehouse in a terrified state and unable to speak. After some assistance from the innkeeper, he was able to tell the crowd that, whilst crossing the village common, he had been confronted by a villager called Dorothy Griffith. The woman was dancing with a number of lit lanterns around her head, rooting him firmly to the spot. The woman then moved away but the lanterns continued to glow and dance. In his opinion, Dorothy Griffith was a witch and should be summoned to remove the curse.

The poor woman was duly summoned and said a blessing to appease the man, who then claimed an instant improvement in his state thus proving that she was a witch. He insisted that she be arrested and placed in prison. The villagers however petitioned that she was not a witch, and that she be set free. The punishment for withcraft at the time was a rather gruesome death but, on close examination, it transpired that William Griffith had long held a grudge against Dorothy Griffith and she was fully pardoned.

# Point of Air Docks

Probably the best-preserved dock on the Dee estuary, Point of Air is sadly no longer in use apart from a few fishermen who operate from here. The property passed to RJB Mining from the National Coal Board in 1994 but the colliery closed in 1996 when the company hit geological faults that stopped them proceeding any further under the Irish Sea. The face at that time was over two and a half miles out under the sea. Rumours abounded that the dock might reopen in connection with the coal trade, but as is often the case, they were nothing more than rumours.

The colliery used its own ships, mainly to carry coal to a coal less Ireland. The colliery also supplied the hungry power stations of Lancashire, over one thousand tonnes a day leaving Point of Air for Fiddlers Ferry Power Station. Witnessing the last coal train leaving Point of Air late one summer's night, with a total of forty-seven coal-trucks – the longest train ever to leave the colliery, was a sad occasion.

Archive records show that the following ships were operational from Point of Air at some time.

| | |
|---|---|
| *Clwyd* | 200 tons; plied coal from Point of Air to Ireland until she was sunk by a German 'U' boat in World War I. |
| *Tanlan* | 293 tons; once owned by Spillers and Millers of Liverpool. She was later one of the Point of Air fleet carrying coal to Ireland. |
| *SS Talacre* | 301 tons; also carried coal to Ireland. She was machine-gunned and badly damaged in World War I, but without any casualties. |

*Point-of-Air*   Previously named *Solway Firth* of Glasgow. 325 tons and used in the coal trade.

Two other ships of interest which worked out of the port were: *Maurita*, sunk by mines off the mouth of the Mersey in World War II and *River Loyne*, which went down off Puffin Island in 1948. One of her oil-lamps was retrieved in a trawl but her sinking remains a mystery.

The name Point of Air is something of a mystery in itself. Cannon Ellis-Davies offers an explanation in his *Flintshire Place Names* of 1959. He believed that Air derived from a similarly sounding Norse word that meant *a gravely bank or a sandy expanse*. This probably refers to the whole Talacre and Point of Air area of the coast where a gravely expanse stretched for many miles in days gone by. There were also vast areas of sand dunes reaching far inland over where the A548 now runs. Time, erosion and alterations to the flood plain during the 18th century removed much of the sand-dune expanse, but much of the gravel remains as it did on the Wirral side of the estuary until the silting covered it. Much of the silting, according to Pennant, was, as a result of the canalization of the Dee. The Welsh name for Point of Air is *Y Parlwr Du.*

# The Dee Ports of the Wirral Peninsula

There are no ports on the Wirral Peninsula today, and little remains to suggest that there ever were any important ports in the area, but this was the main point of embarkation to Ireland for troops and for general trading from the north-west.

The strip from Denhall to Hoylake was known in older documents as the *Neston Anchorage*. The ports listed on the *Neston Anchorage* were Beerhouse Hole, Beer House, Parkgate, Moorside, New Quay and Ness Colliery Quay. The entire Wirral peninsula however was known as *Chester Water*, and this presents considerable problems. Many records show that cargoes moved in or out of the *Chester Water*, but exact ports are not named. Also, much of the over-all tonnage is generalised as being from *Chester Water*.

Beer House was a public house which stood at the bottom end of Boathouse Lane in Parkgate, but the anchorage for Beer House was thought to be a sandy mooring some 1,000 yards lower down the estuary. Some historians think that this may have been the start of Parkgate. In the 17th century, when there were few houses in the locality, it was spelt *Birhouse.*

Burton is mentioned as a small port from around 1357 and records show that large numbers of millstones arrived here by sea from Anglesey. Also, large numbers of archers were dispatched from here to Ireland in 1399. By 1480 however, merchants using Burton complained that charges were too high, and petitioned the Crown for help. A bad payment scheme was in force resulting in many ships being impounded because of debt, their cargoes being handed to the Mayor of Chester. If the Mayor accepted the cargo, the ship must lie untouched for forty days at anchor. The system was flawed and much cargo rotted in the holds. As with all the ports on the Wirral, owners complained that in rough weather, ships at anchor in the ports received more damage than if they'd been left to ride out the storm, this being the west-facing side of the peninsula. Anchorage was itself a problem as most of the ports on the smaller tides were nothing better than a ship grounded on soft sand, and its cargo being humped to the shoreline. To improve matters a stone pier was built below Neston Parish Church, running out into the estuary.

In 1689 there were over ten thousand men camped near Neston waiting to cross to Ireland given clement weather. They were part of Cromwell's force and there are many subsequent accounts of the merciless manner in which they carried out their duties, slaughtering women and children begging for mercy, all in the name of their favoured creed.

Neston had her shipbuilding programme and also a ship repair programme The Royal Yachts frequently called here to have their sides cleaned in the 18th century. It is thought that the first ship to be built on the Wirral was *Exchange*, of 90 tons, in 1701. The brig *Minerva* at 100 tons, six guns, and a crew of eleven men, was a regular from the Wirral to Marseilles carrying a cargo of lead. Her return cargo was fresh fruit, which would probably be contaminated by lead should it not be over ripe by the time it arrived on the Wirral.

There was so much trade through Neston in the mid to late 18th century that a customs house was built here. Inns began to appear on the front, making a roaring trade when ships failed to get away in bad weather. There was also a lively trade with the Welsh ports. Customs men had a rough time on the Wirral, with piracy being described as 'big business' between France and Spain and the Wirral ports, especially Neston. There was also a thriving 'black-market' between France and the Wirral in port, wines, lace and other luxury goods, especially tobacco. It was so fierce that the customs men of Neston were allowed to shoot first and ask questions after.

The composer George Frideric Handel is said to have left Neston for

Ireland in 1741 having visited St Werburgh's, Chester, seeking choristers for his *Messiah*, but he left disappointed. Whilst in Neston he stayed at the 'St George', which was later Mostyn School.

Ireland has no coal deposits of its own and much Welsh coal left Neston to Ireland. Some reports claimed that the Welsh coal sent over was of a poor quality and too quick burning. Indeed, at one time there was a problem in transporting sufficient coal there.

Parkgate had a big deer-park, built by Roger de Montalt, builder of Mold Castle. Possibly the first proper building in the area was the keeper's lodge for the park. The land was sold in 1599 to the Earl of Derby and it is thought that a small settlement arose. Prior to this time it was known simply as Neston Park.

As a port, Parkgate soon got into full swing and a licence was granted for the export and sale of calfskin to Ireland. By the early 17th century this was the most important trading port on the Neston Anchorage. Trade was very much governed by the weather and there were times when traders and ships were laid-up for three weeks or more because of inclement conditions. By the 18th century it was described as 'every bit as dangerous as Holy Head and as poor to shipping'.

Parkgate took ships up to 400 tons, some on the Atlantic trade. In the Civil War it was important for troop movements from Ireland. It was from here that Oliver Cromwell sailed to create total carnage at Drogheda (Droched Atha). The first passenger service from Parkgate to Ireland probably came in 1615, but the travelling public had to share a ship with the military and their horses. The sea captains feared a ship full of horses because panic could spread like wildfire. There is a disturbing tale of a ship rolling badly in rough weather with forty or more horses on board. The captain feared that the ship might be lost, so gave the order to cut the throats of the more troublesome horses, thus saving the ship. This was a regular if gruesome practise on ships in the 17th and 18th centuries.

As the trade from Parkgate increased, so did the number of inns and hotels offering accommodation to travellers waiting for the wind to change. Most of these buildings, it is said, had a purpose built cellar often full of contraband, waiting to be moved under the cover of darkness.

The Beer House ports were out of use by 1740. The canalization scheme and the training walls moved the main channel to the Welsh side of the estuary and the Wirral ports declined. Most could only be used on bigger tides but Parkgate, the main port on the Wirral, continued. Lighthouses were erected on the Wirral at Leasowe (1763), Hoylake (1764) and Bidston (1771).

The lighthouse at Leasowe is claimed to be one of the earliest in

England. It was built in 1764 on land bought for £42 per square yard, and was used for guiding ships into both the Dee and the Mersey estuaries. It closed in 1908. It is still used by seafarers for navigation today, being preserved as a historical landmark.

In 1775 two ships were lost out of Parkgate, resulting in pilots having to be licensed on the river. The two ships were *Trevor* under Captain William Tatty and *Nonpariel* under Captain Davies. It appears that the military placed considerable pressure on Captain Davies to put to sea against his better judgement. He related his fears to others including his wife. The ship went down with the loss of one hundred lives, including forty-three vagrants from the Neston House of Correction. *Nonpariel* grounded on the Hoyle Bank in the Dee estuary mouth and the bodies and much of her cargo was washed ashore onto the Welsh side of the estuary. Nineteen people were arrested in the Fflint area for robbing the dead. *Trevor* was carrying £6,000 worth of silks, jewels and linen in a cargo that exceeded £40,000 when she foundered off the coast of Lancashire.

The *Gentlemans Magazine* dated 14.9.1806 records a ship out of Parkgate bound for Ireland foundering on the Hoyle Bank. Out of one hundred persons on board just three survived. At the time there were four sailings a week to Ireland.

Chester City Archives has an interesting photograph of the foreshore at Meols taken about 1910, showing tree stumps from a forest that once covered the foreshore. A *Gentlemans Magazine* dated 1796 refers to the heavy forestry that came down to the foreshore on both sides of the estuary, saying that the trees came well into the sea flow area. It excites the mind to think of the hey-day of smuggling, with a rising tide among trees resemble mangrove at the edge of the Amazonian forest, and small boats full of brandy or tobacco trying to avoid the customs men.

Hoylake is now an attractive tourist centre with marinas and surfing areas. In the 18th century it had a large area of sand dunes, much as Point of Air. The dunes were protected by law and anyone found disturbing them, or grazing the grasses that held the dunes together, were in grave danger of going to gaol because the dunes formed a natural anti-flood barrier. In those days there were no mountain bikes or scramblers to desecrate the coasts, as is happening today at Talacre.

Hoylake had a fair trade with the Welsh ports, mostly in coal to Ireland but this stopped in 1909 when it became impossible to get big ships to the quayside because of the increased silting.

Following the running down of Shotwick quay after canalization, its trade moved up the estuary to Parkgate. During the reign of Elizabeth I

Shotwick port was enlarged (1533-1603) and new stone quays were built to aid shipping. Following the Civil War, they were taken down by Sir Roger Mostyn and used as part of the sea defences at Parkgate.

In nearby Ness in the year 1765 a daughter, named Emma Lyon, was born to the village blacksmith. Despite the relative poverty and limitation of her upbringing, she carved herself a place on the edges of history by becoming the mistress of Lord Nelson. She obtained employment in London and, in 1782, became the mistress of Charles Greville. In 1786 she became mistress to Sir William Hamilton (1730-1803) the British Envoy at Naples. She was said to be a leading figure in Neapolitan society, and Hamilton made an honest woman of her in 1791. When Nelson returned from the Nile in 1798 she became his mistress, bearing him a daughter in 1801. Following the deaths of both Hamilton and Nelson, it seems that the dear lady fell heavily into debt and was imprisoned. She escaped to the port of Calais where she died in real poverty.

Ness is now known worldwide for its gardens and its furtherance of endangered species of plants. The gardens are open to the public and are sign-posted off the A41.

A curious phenomenon occurred one morning in the spring of 1927, when the morning tide failed to arrive at all. It reached a point near Hoylake, but no further. It is an oft-told story that is rarely believed, but it did actually happen. Scientific studies show that, on the previous days, there had been a very severe gale out in the Irish Sea, followed by a violent change in direction of the winds. This was strong enough to create an oscillation that effectively held back the tide, so that only a weak surge occurred that died soon after entering the estuary.

# Shotwick

This is a delightful village well off the main route on the Wirral. It is visited by only the keenest of walkers these days who have made an in-depth study of their OS map, or who got lost. A traveller arriving here by car might well be forgiven for thinking this is the place that time forgot.

Shotwick boasts a delightful church that dates back as far as the 11th century, although all that remains of the original building is the porchway. Even that has a 16th century door hung in it, although it has a most interesting locking system. Marks on the stone work of the seating in the porch are said to have been made by archers, sharpening their arrows. Others are far more mundane, saying that they are the marks of maintenance staff sharpening their tools for trimming the grass. It is quite possible that the former is true since there was a point below Shotwick where raiding parties from Wales frequently crossed to steal the fat Wirral livestock. The Wirral men would not have allowed their cattle across without a little demonstration of displeasure.

The church is as attractive from the inside as the outside. Six bells peal out calling the faithful to worship, being rung from the ground floor level. The hand-carved pews are of the boxed-in type so common in many of the older churches in southern England. Some have nameplates indicating the power of the landed gentry at a time when a family could buy a pew for their exclusive use. Many vicars allowed it, but others were braver. A terrible row occurred at Mold Parish Church in the 1950's. A supposedly noble family had it explained to them by the vicar that the parish magazine's front page had a statement to the effect that 'All seats were free in the Church'.

An unusual feature of the church is the placing of the churchwarden's pew at the rear of the congregation – today occupied by a lady churchwarden. It is an old canopied seat bearing the dates 1673-1709. In days gone by, churchwardens would wear long wigs and many smoked a clay-pipe reaching almost to their waist. They would cast a judgmental eye over who attended and who did not.

The graveyard contains the remains of many families that had connections with the sea, although many captions on the headstones are no longer visible. Near the Chancel is a flat tombstone bearing something that resembles a pair of stirrups and a bridle-bit, dated 1187. The story goes that Squire Hockenhull of Shotwick Manor was thrown to the ground when his horse tripped in a rabbit-hole. Before he died he instructed his son to carve a bridle-bit and two stirrups on his tombstone, rather than an inscription. However the will of John Carter, curate of Shotwick who departed this earth in 1587, shows that he requested to be buried within the church. Recent research suggests that the carved bit and stirrups could well be mistaken for the more ornamental JCC (John Carter Curate), and that the date be 1587 rather than 1187. Who knows?

The perimeter wall is a matter of controversy because some stones have rotting iron rings attached to them, and many have traces of rings already rotted away. There is a belief that this wall was once part of the quayside that Shotwick is known to have once had and that ships would have been tied here. But there are no positive records that the Dee lapped the churchyard wall as is commonly supposed, and a more likely story is that when Shotwick castle was demolished its stones were used here, being a ready cut supply of quality cut stone. Holt castle suffered the same fate when Eaton Hall was built in Chester.

The Shotwick Yews have long disappeared from near the church. They were used extensively for spears and arrows. The two fields below the church are marked on the old tithe map of 1843 as *The Butts*. It is supposed that it was here that the English/Norman soldiers tried out their weapons before engaging the Welsh in battle, having crossed the ford that ran from the bottom of the lane adjacent to the church across the estuary.

This ford had much use as it was safer, if wetter, than running the gauntlet of the highwaymen operating between Chester and the Wirral. It was in use until the 18th century. The grassy lane that leads the visitor past the church ends abruptly. It is assumed that this occurred after the Dee changed course. The lane is known as *The Olde Saltesway*, suggesting a strong maritime connection.

The ford was used for many illicit journeys bearing wines, spirits and tobacco to and from the Wirral. The lonely shoreline from Mostyn to Talacre was as well known a haunt for smugglers as was Hilbre Island. Next to Shotwick vicarage there is a large house with false-floors. Smugglers and other refugees from the law hid here and probably their booty too, until it was safe to move on.

Shotwick was a rival to Gretna Green during the second half of the 17th century. A certain Ralph Heath was brought before the Bishop's Court in 1674 for unseemly behaviour, which was probably supplementing his measly earnings as a schoolmaster.

Shotwick has a legend of its own and, like many others, there are different versions to it. The gist goes something like this. On Hilbre Island is a place called 'Lady's Cave', where a Benedictine monk dwelt. One day he found a young woman dying on the foreshore, having been cast up by the sea. Before she died she told the monk that she was the only daughter of the custodian of Shotwick castle and, against her father's wishes, had fallen in love with one of his enemies. Her father however had arranged that she marry a man of his choice – a Welsh knight called Llywelyn. On discovering her secret, her father sent her packing to marry Llywelyn. But, whilst crossing the treacherous Dee estuary, the boat capsized and she was left to the mercy of the sea. Either that or she threw herself overboard. Sadly, after relating her story to the monk, she died.

The castle at Shotwick is now no more than a few stones protruding from a green field but, prior to the canalization of the Dee in the 18th century, it stood on the shores of the Dee and was a major port on the Dee. It is thought that the land to build the castle was given by Hugh Lupus, first Earl of Chester. Its position was ideally suited as it guarded a crossing of the old river at a place that could be forded at low water. Built of stone amd possibly with six towers, one of which was reputed to be over five stories tall, it remained important until well into the 14th century.

Henry II came to Shotwick and planned his assaults on the Welsh from here. The Welsh rose in full rebellion against the Normans in 1256, ,forcing their way right up to Chester. The Earl of Chester, on seeing what he estimated as being an army in excess of 30,000 troops, fled the city, and Shotwick castle saw some proper acton.

Henry III (1207-1272) and his wife also stayed at Shotwick. It was here that Henry decided that the Welsh were not a nation to give in easy, and it was from here that he planned further military attacks. Llywelyn for his part refused to pay homage to the Norman/English Crown. In 1280, Edward I came here and bestowed knighthoods on those who had followed him against the Welsh. He left Shotwick by boat for Rhuddlan with his principal engineer. In the lists of 1331 Shotwick castle was included as one of those to be regularly inspected and repaired as necessary, such was its importance. The dock adjacent to the castle was used to ship stone to rebuild Chester in the 14th century.

During the reign of Elizabeth I (1533-1603) many thousands of troops left Shotwick for Ireland, and it may have been used during Cromwell's cruel purges in Ireland. Silting was becoming a severe problem and the Neston anchorages became a better proposition for getting troops, horses and provisions away to Ireland. Slowly, people began to move down the estuary and Shotwick became less and less important. At the end of the 16th century the castle was granted to Sir Hugh Calveley and it was officially classed as a ruin by 1607. When the Dee was canalized in the 18th century, Shotwick was no longer near the river.

During the reclamation of the Dee in the 18th century it is thought that what was left of the castle was used as sea defences. Also some of it, probably the dock, appears in the exterior wall of Shotwick church.

According to Ormerod's *History of Cheshire*, the Shotwick hall stood at the rear of the church. Shotwick was possessed by the secular canons of St Werburgh's in Chester before the Norman Conquest.

# Hilbre Islands

There are three Hilbre Islands situated off the Wirral Peninsula. They can be easily reached on low water by walking across the sands. It is said that there was a natural causeway from the islands to the mainland, though nothing remains of it today due to erosion, the islands having a sandstone base. The islands have been inhabited for a very long time, the highest population probably being around twenty people. Norse settlers came to the Wirral and probably used the islands. The Romans may have used them as a catapult station to defend the estuary. Neolithic arrowheads have been found there, and a Bronze axe-head recovered from there was made in Ireland. Cremated remains found there could also be Bronze Age.

There has been a religious settlement on Hilbre possibly as far back as 905. In Norman times the islands were given to the Abbey of St Erroul in Normandy, but later passed to St Werburgh's Abbey (Chester). In 1522 there was a cell on Hilbre dedicated to St Mary the Virgin, resulting in a long line of pilgrims paying homage to the island. Little is known of the ac:ual monastics on the island but there were possibly two, a monk and helperThe Abbey maintained them until its dissolution in 1541, when they came under the control of Chester Cathedral.

. In 1232 the Earl of Chester made an allowance of 10/- per annum for lighting on Hilbre, this probably for lighting the altar. The monks were responsible for collecting tithes from the Wirral on behalf of St Werburgh. The religious connection was probably in place until the 19th century when the island came under the control of the Dean and Chapter of Chester and the Liverpool Dock Trustees.

In 1495 one John Lancaster of Hilbre was charged with taking a *thirpole* (porpoise) valued at 100 shillings and the property of the Crown. Both porpoise and sturgeon are 'royal' fish, the Crown having first claim on any caught. The last monk recorded leaving Hilbre, in 1538, was Robert Wyngham (Wiggan) described as 'Prior of the Cell of Hilbre'. He duly received a pension of £6 per year. A Celtic sandstone cross found in a broken state was long used as a gate-stop until it was identified, and now lies in Chester museum.

Because of the deeper water off Hilbre, ships often loaded and unloaded there rather than lie out on the sands off the Wirral anchorage. Goods were moved along planks to and from horse and cart. Ships using Hilbre took a variety of locally made wares out, mostly to Ireland. Incoming ships had cargoes of hides for the important tanning industry in Chester.

Records for 1565/6 show that 38,500 Brockfelles (Badger skins) came to Hilbre and 30,950 shepe felles (sheep-skins). In 1581 pirates off Holyhead, Anglesey, seized the Margaret. Piracy was always a threat, and was often deadly. Survivors of the *Margaret* describe the attacking ship as 'a tall barque with two tops in a very warlike manner'.

The ship *Jesus* is recorded as taking cloth to Ireland on 8 October 1565 and returning with hides and salt. Within seven days she was out again fully loaded. There is a record of a ship leaving Hilbre bound for Bilbao in Spain being attacked and boarded off Anglesey. She was released and allowed to continue on her journey. On the return journey to Hilbre pirates again attacked her and the cargo was this time stolen. Pirates hung another ship's captain from the yards of his own vessel.

The *Katrina of Chester* left Hilbre for Dublin with a cargo of two horses sent to 'The Kyng's Grove' and two cases of 'gentle hawks', these probably being peregrine falcons. A person was seen as someone of high status if they hunted hawks, and the type of hawk rated their superiority. A peregrine was of a high status, whilst a sparrow hawk was used by under-classes.

During the reign of Elizabeth I, Hilbre was used extensively as a base from where troops and horses and other armaments were dispatched for Ireland. In later years Oliver Cromwell used Hilbre for the same purpose. In more recent times trips were available to north Wales for 6d per person from Hilbre and some of the Wirral ports, depending on the tide.

There are unconfirmed reports that Hilbre was used as a trap for shipping. The claims, although unsubstantiated, were that a light was placed in a window of the public house on Hilbre, and used to 'aid' shipping on the treacherous estuary at night. The ships steered by the light, only to be grounded on the mud-banks. People waiting on the islands then relieved the ships of their cargoes. Little is known of this activity but there are records of Customs men using nearby Red Rocks to observe the estuary.

Cargoes were of high quality wines, spirit, tobacco, linen and other goods destined for the British market. It is widely suspected that the smuggling operations were overseen by the local gentry on both the English and Welsh side of the river. Detection was very poor and the freedom with which the smugglers operated so openly suggests, they had few fears. The gentry were also the law in those times and ran the courts.

A Doctor Leigh and some of his friends started a 'Boilery of Salt' on Hilbre in 1670 to boil down rock salt from Northwich. It was shipped to Hilbre for boiling. The company leased the islands from Chester Cathedral on a twenty-one year lease at 2/6d per year. They spent £1,640 on the project and had plans to enlarge the business to eight boiling plants. Unfortunately, the business foundered after the partners fell out.

In 1774 a William Penkett and several partners attempted to start oyster farming off Hilbre. The idea met stiff opposition from the Mayor of Hoylake and local ship owners who claimed, falsely, that the oysters would cling to the ships anchor chains causing problems, and could be a danger to shipping. The idea was abandoned. A second attempt was made in 1879. This attempt did not endure as much opposition but it failed because the Liverpool market claimed that the oysters were of 'too poor a quality'. Also many oysters disappeared for unknown reasons. This attempt was also abandoned.

Hilbre was prominent in both World Wars. In World War I there were twenty-one men stationed on the islands throughout the duration of the war in case Ireland fell to the Germans. In World War II a machine-gun section was placed on the islands to defend the estuary, but they were not much troubled.

Today Hilbre is a tourist attraction and can be reached from the Wirral on foot at low water. It is controlled and expertly run by The Wirral Country Park and there is a resident warden living on the island. It is a noted bird-watching paradise and each month at high-water, a bird count takes place as the birds rest up on the rocks awaiting the tide to recede so they can feed again.

# Shipbuilding on the river Dee

The Romans were the first to build a ship of any size on the Dee, their boatyard probably being at the Roodeye, Chester. It was not until medieval times however that serious boat building began, although it did not become a substantial industry at Chester until the 18th century. The plentiful hardwoods of north Wales, Delamere and imports some from America were used.

The City Assembly has minutes showing that land was let for the purpose of shipbuilding on the Roodeye from 1740, but only on a small scale. It was not until the canalization of the river that shipbuilding was of much commercial importance. Records show that from the 18th century a total of four hundred and fifty ships were built on the Dee but the actual number is thought to have been in excess of that. Even that number was outstripping Merseyside at that time. There is also a reference in the City Assembly minutes to the effect that damage was being caused to the Roodeye by shipbuilding as early as 1680, but little seems to have been done. At this time despite the poor state of the river, ships of some considerable size were being built, like the *Lord Forbes* (at 556 tons) for a Liverpool firm. Following canalization shipyards sprang-up along the entire length of the tidal reaches of the Dee, most of them on the Welsh side which was less exposed and nearer to a road, and later the railway system. The more exposed English side of the river had a yard at

Parkgate and it is said that one of the first ships built on the Dee, called 'Ferret', may have been at that yard.

At Chester the Roodeye yard was initially operated by John & Joseph Troughton, part of the yard being where at the Chester Gas works site. It was later operated by Jacksons and then taken over by William Courtney.

William Courtney was then one of the more important names on the river Dee. In 1804 they built two twelve gun Brigantines of 178 tons for the Navy and four more in 1815 – HMS *Cyrus*, HMS *Mersey*, HMS *Eden* (she weighed 451 tons and carried twenty-four guns), HMS *Levant* (had twenty-six guns and weighed 464 tons). Courtney's operated from the 'River Dee Company Yard' from about 1800 until roughly 1820.

Troughtons also operated from the 'River Dee Company Yard' on the Roodeye from about 1783 until 1818. They built paddle steamers, including the *St George* (605 tons), built especially for the India trade. It was said that she was fast and could make Madras and back in under twelve months. Apparently this yard came to an end sometime in 1845 when a spark from a passing train set it alight. The property was destroyed and never rebuilt.

Shipbuilding was a prosperous affair at Fflint for many decades, Ferguson & Baird going there in the 1840's to build big ships near the castle. They built two and three mast schooners at Flint and enjoyed a good trade in steel from Brymbo. The shipbuilders moved higher up river to Connah's Quay when the chemical works, which had been built on part of the castle, wished to expand. Ferguson & Baird continued shipbuilding at Connah's Quay until 1916 when Chrichton's bought them out. They closed in 1930.

By the 19th century yards were springing up along the length of the Dee as far as Point of Air, the river boasting a total of fourteen shipbuilders during the 19th and 20th centuries.

| | |
|---|---|
| Talacre | John Dawson (1838-1848) |
| Mostyn | Edward Eyton (1838-1848) |
| | Thomas Mathias (1848-?) |
| Bagillt | Chester Lead Company (1841-1863) |
| Fflint | David Jones (1849-1881) |
| | Ferguson & Baird (1852-1858) |
| Connah's Quay | Ferguson & Baird (1858-1910) (following a move from Fflint as their land was required for an extension of a chemical works) |
| | J Crichton & Co (1910-1935) |
| Queensferry | James Boydell (1836-1840) |

| | |
|---|---|
| | Abdela & Mitchell (1908-1938) |
| Sandycroft | John Rigby (1830-1852) which then became |
| | George Cramm (1852-1856) |
| Saltney | J Crichton & Co (1913-1935) |
| Lower Basin (Chester) | William Roberts (1890-1916) |
| Chester Roodeye | John Troughton (1783-1818) |
| | John Wilson (1828–?) |
| | Wm Beshton (1855-1865) |
| River Dee Co Yard | Peter Jackson (1767-1800) |
| | Wm Courtney (1800-1820) |
| | Wm Mulvey (1820-1852) |
| | George Cramm (1852-1856) |
| | Cox & Miller (1857-1869) |
| Neston | Thomas Makin (c. 1787-1791) |

Ferguson & Baird and David Jones all built ships of very high quality as did the other yards, but one of the most famous yards on the Dee was the Sandycroft yard of John Rigby (1830-1852), this being the 'Sandycroft Iron Foundry Yard'. They built paddle steamers and one of the best known was the *Forth*. The yard was purchased by George Cramm in 1852. Cramm had been deeply impressed by the new side-launching method he had seen on the Mersey and began to experiment with iron-ships on the Dee, using the side-launch method. His first ship was the *Amelia* of 350 tons, first built at Chester in 1853 as *Winifred*. Then came the most written about of all Dee ships – *The Royal Charter*.

Sensation and mystery surrounded the ship from the moment she was laid down and the mystery still exists today. The keel was laid down at Cramms Yard, Sandycroft. She was an iron ship designed by J Grinrod for Charles Moore & Co of Liverpool. She was lengthened by stretching both ends, giving the ship an overall length of some 336 feet and a gross tonnage of 2,076 tons. A beam of 40' 6" was retained. Not long after the keel had been laid she was sold to Gibbs, Bright & Co who were then operating the Liverpool to Melbourne run under 'The Liverpool & Australian Steam Navigation Company'.

The Australian gold rush was on at the time and everybody wanted to get away to make a fortune. The need for ships was high as passages to Australia were in such a demand. The company already had the *Great Britain*, but another ship was badly needed as well as several other sailing-packets. There was considerable pressure to find a ship that would complete the Australia run in sixty days or less. The partly built Royal Charter was purchased amid the panic and pressure of the time.

Following her loss, accusations were made that her hull had not been properly built, or there was a design fault that should have been corrected, but this was disproved at a later date. She lies at the bottom of the sea in a most inaccessible place due to dangerous currents. Even modern day divers can only visit the wreck during certain times, and on certain heights of the tide.

Her anchors weighed 51 cwts (2590kg) each and were made at Woods Chain Works at Saltney. There were rumours that there may have been defects in the chains, but tests have disproved this as samples were tested to 72 tons. Prior to this however, there was a lack of legislation requiring the testing of chains, thus the 'Anchor and Cables Act 1863' came into force.

*Royal Charter* was a fully rigged three-mast ship with 15,000 square-feet of sail. She was an early version of recently introduced ships with a split topsail for easier handling. The ropes were made of wire at Queensferry and her masts were of wood. She had a top speed of 14 knots and reduced the journey from Melbourne to fifty-nine days.

George Cramm called in the liquidators in August 1854 and the *Royal Charter* was finished by others. She was ready to be launched in July 1855. On July 31 at 12 noon the tide was full and the scene set for her launching by Mrs Gibbs, wife of one of the owners. The bottle was swung, the band played and everyone clapped. But half way down the slipway she jammed tight and, despite the assistance of three tugs, she refused to move any further. It was said that the tallow (animal fats) used to grease the runners had melted in the heat of high summer, and so jammed her hull. She was to be left until August 28, the next big tide. But without explanation, and fuelling the minds of the fortune-tellers of doom and gloom, a few nights prior to the 28th she slid another forty-feet towards the water before jamming again. There was no reasonable explanation for the movement, adding to the tales of woe. However, on August 28 she got away, doubtless to more clapping and more brass bands. The panic was over.

It seems that every one heaved their collective sigh of relief a little too soon for, at a point near Fflint, she grounded again on a sand-bank. There she lay, stuck for another month until the next high-tide. Tugs were blamed for losing her and all manner of accusations bounded about, but it seems that the age old problem of the channel shifting had stopped her, and there was little that man could have done.

She was freed a month later and went straight into Liverpool dry-dock without further recorded problems. Examination of her hull showed that damage had been caused to her plates, and considerable strengthening work had to be done before she could get away again. It was February

1856 before she went into service, proving a great success with both the public and the crews. But on August 26, 1859 she foundered off Moelfre and was lost forever along with hundreds of souls.

It was said at the enquiry that, on the night she went down, the worst storm in living memory was raging. Winds of hitherto unknown proportions were blowing, and the seas were of a record height.

Whatever the cause, it signalled the end of the Sandycroft yard although it was later taken-over by Cox & Miller. They built some big ships including *Gitana* (1,366 tons), *Roodeye* (1,036 tons) and *Robinson Crusoe* at (1,163 tons).

By the end of the 19th century only Ferguson & Baird remained at Connah's Quay. They were bought out by the firm of J Crichton's, as was a Saltney yard in 1913. They built some spectacular ships – tugboats, paddle steamers, trawlers, barges and floating-grain-stores made with a very shallow-draught for the shallows of foreign countries. This yard closed in 1935. Their biggest ship was the *Allegheny* at 856 tons. Their yard in Connah's Quay is today the wood-yard of Musgraves, adjacent to the 'Old Quay House' on Connah's Quay docks.

The ships built by Ferguson, McCullum & Baird at Fflint were mostly wooden ones – three-mast schooners for local traders, all of them highly desirable craft.

Since there was no legal obligation to register ships prior to 1785, the record of ships built on Deeside is incomplete. Abdella & Mitchell of Gloucestershire opened the Queensferry yard and built small steamers, including motor-coasters, for John Summers the iron makers of Deeside. Among the ships they made is the *Indorita*, which plied the coasts of Britain and Ireland. Despite her being something of a local personality on Deeside, she was broken up in 1975.

Abdella & Mitchell was the last major yard on the river. Apart from the ships they built for the iron and steelworks, there was the *Menai* working between Caernarfon and Anglesey for many years. She was a paddle steamer. The firm finished trading just before the outbreak of World War II and with them went the last in a long line of shipbuilders on the Dee.

Grasses now grow over slipways, and the stench of pitch and tallow is no more. Old men who knew nothing other than shipbuilding sat down in the warm sunshine of the summer of 1939, smoking pipes and wondering. Never again would bands play; no more would crowds cheer and taut chains clank as gleaming ships slid quietly into the murk of the river Dee. With the last ship and the last echo of a band went an era – it has never returned.

# Tragedies recorded on the river Dee

It is only in recent times that records of tragedies on rivers and estuaries have been kept. The Welsh Dee estuary is a very dangerous place and because of its importance and business, it is inevitable that accidents will occur occasionally. Admiralty charts of the estuary and the north Wales coastline show several wrecks, many marked by Trinity House buoys. The circumstances of many of the very old wrecks are not recorded. People who work on or use the estuary will tell you that, even on the mildest of days, the seemingly tranquil waters, and especially the exposed sands, should always be treated with great respect.

When the estuary was alive with sail-ships the problem of ever shifting sandbanks often caused ships to ground, and no blame could be attached to either the pilot or captain. Ships racing each other into the estuary were another reason for grounding and captains and/or pilots were always fully responsible. It would also be irresponsible to fight against bad crosswinds or attempt to come-up on a falling tide, but it was a mistake that many made.

When grounded, crewmen and captains were known to drop over the side after the tide had fallen-back, attempting to walk to the shoreline. Several experienced men stepped into quicksand, never to be seen. Survivors of such incidents tell of hard sand suddenly gurgling and turning into a wet, oily looking death trap. Someone would cry 'Help' before slithering for ever into the sand, which would then return to its hard state. I had a close shave near Talacre lighthouse one sunny afternoon. Having examined the deposits left by the last tide I noticed that the next tide had began to run up the estuary. It wasn't very close and I felt safe as I walked slowly back towards my family by the dunes. Suddenly the sands went dark as seawater gurgled and mini-whirlpools appeared. Thick black silt oozed out making my attempts to get away from the area very difficult as my shoes sank. Soon I was calf-deep in the stinking silt but managed to struggle out with my Labrador, escaping covered in mud and very afraid. We survived but the Coroner's books are full of those who did not. With the increase in windsurfing and sailing on the estuary it is a matter of time before more pages are added to the Coroner's notes.

Gerry Vernon a pilot from Mostyn and all his life a sailor, recorded that captains forbade crewmembers from dropping over the side should a ship ground. No matter how firm the sands looked they stayed on board until the next tide, which usually lifted them clear. It was often difficult to persuade the crews within sight of the port or dry land, but it had to be done – the record books dictated such a policy.

The first recorded drowning on the Dee was of a Roman officer awaiting promotion. It is thought that he drowned from a fishing vessel, and a stone commemorating his death can now be seen at Chester museum. It is thought that the body was never recovered, the inscription remaining unfinished for that reason.

There must have been numerous deaths in the many centuries before the Romans came to Chester, and many more than the unfortunate officer must have died in the river during their occupation. The only record of the officer's death was a fortunate find from an archaeological dig, but the records remained quiet for a very long time after the Romans. One might safely assume that the legend of the keeper of Shotwick Castle was nothing more than a fireside story from a cold, windy night.

Until Kinderley changed the course of the river in the 18th century, it must have been a dreadful place to cross. Many used the crossings, including drovers, cattle thieves, traders, smugglers, soldiers and all manner of humanity. The toll on man, beast and goods must have been high.

Clwyd Archives Office at Hawarden has in its possession a book from the Mostyn estate at Talacre, containing all manner of stories of wrecks and deaths by drowning off the foreshore under the control of Mostyn Hall. One Hugh Spencer penned much of the book. (See Appendix 1).

The pilot boats were long strong wooden boats with a crew of perhaps six rowing and one attending to the oil-lamps hung astern. The pilot's task was often death defying, especially when seas were rough and unfamiliar ships needed assistance. Watching the modern day pilot leaving Mostyn in his self-righting unsinkable orange boat gives one a little more perspective of the hazards the seamen of old faced.

The summoner of the Coroner from Mold, who travelled on horseback at all hours for the sum of 1/4d, was a busy man. So were the farmers and their heavy horses, needed to pull wrecks and masts ashore. In this area people who pulled bodies from the sea were also paid a sum of money, although this practise was not adopted in all coastal areas. This coastline was sparsely populated and yet as soon as bad weather blew-up someone would be watching for ships in distress. The 'local people' knew when they were on to a winner.

# Crossing, and the canalization of, the lower Dee

Along the course of the river Dee, most bridges are erected at, or near to, a ford where drovers, carts and pedestrians always crossed the river. The Old Dee Bridge at Chester has been a crossing point for pedestrians and livestock since Roman times, its suitability being obvious at low-water when the bed is exposed. On the tidal reaches this ford was the nearest to Chester, whilst the next was at Saltney, although it crossed a difficult path through the marshes, coming out where Blacon is today, and could only be crossed at low water. The next crossing point was roughly where the old Ferry road-bridge now stands at Queensferry, and the last one was from somewhere near Fflint to Shotwick.

The first boats of any size to use the lower river were the Roman troop-ships heading for Chester, although they recorded their displeasure at the silting and the ever changing channel. The Romans are thought to have erected a wooden light-tower somewhere on the estuary to assist shipping. It would have been a barrel of pitch that was set alight.

A report that appeared in 1377 described the 'ruineth state of the river that preventeth ships approaching the City walls of Chester.' There was a similar report in 1485,and another in the early 16th century. A 17th century report by Andrew Yarrington called the *English Improvement by Sea and Land* states:

> 'In the month of July 1674 I was prevailed with a person of honour to survey the river Dee, running from the City of Chester to the Irish Sea, and finding the river choked with sand so that a vessel of some 20 tons could not come up to that noble city, and the ships were forced to lie-up at Neston, in a very bad place. In the harbour the ships did receive much damage and trade made so uncertain and changeable that the trade of Chester is much decayed and gone to Liverpool and that old great city is in danger of being ruined.'

The publication of the report acted as a stimulus to the rulers of the City, and the citizens demanded something be done. In 1684 Captain Grenville Collins, hydrographer to the navy and king, was commissioned to carry out an in-depth survey into the state of the Dee. On the strength of this, the citizens and the Mayor of Chester sought an Act of Parliament in 1700 to ensure that the river was maintained at a navigable depth of ten or eleven feet, so that ships of 100 tons might come up to the city on high-water.

The Act required that a channel be maintained and authorised the City of Chester to levy charges on ships in the river. It was to be enforced for at least twenty-one years. Still nothing was done, mainly for a lack of finance.

In 1732 one John Mackay, a mathematician, made a further survey. His chart showed a channel running under Shotwick and Burton point, alongside Parkgate. It also showed that the channel varied in depth from 2 feet at low water to 20 feet on a spring tide. The figure for Burton was 7 and 19 feet; Saltney had 2 and 10 feet while Chester could only boast 2 and 9 feet. The report added that, unless something positive was done, Chester port would cease to exist as the silt was getting out of control, stopping bigger ships from reaching the city. It was decided that a new port should be built at Neston to cope with the silting, with goods transferred to Chester by road or flat-bottomed boats.

By 1737, tolls from shipping had dropped by as much as one-third as ships failed to reach Chester. The City Fathers had been discussing the problem for almost forty years but nothing had been done, or looked like being done. Traders, warehouses and anyone connected with the port all suffered. Demands were made that action be taken before Chester port ceased to exist.

The pressure made the City Fathers seek a further Act of Parliament, this time to alter the course of the river. Nathaniel Kinderley, a Lincolnshire man, was asked to give his opinion on the problem. His plan was simple: dig a straight new canal from Saltney out to sea giving a maximum depth of sixteen feet on a moderate tide. The earth that was removed was to be used as banking on either side of the canal. An added benefit was that land reclamation would be possible to the extent that in excess of 2,000 acres would come into agricultural use. Kinderley's plan was strongly supported, although some seriously opposed it on the grounds that water flow would be reduced, lessening the scouring-out of the estuary, meaning that the silt would still remain.

The new canal would be from just below Saltney to below New Quay (Connah's Quay). It was to be 3¼ miles long, commencing 2½ miles below Chester. The river was turned in to the cut in 1737 and the task of reclaiming the land on either side began. It was another fifty years before it became a paying proposition for the Dee Company, that had bought Kinderley's share. The channel itself at first varied from 660 feet wide at Chester to 1,500 feet wide at Connah's Quay and they soon experienced difficulty in maintaining the channel below Queensferry and Connah's Quay. The channel also began to settle on the Welsh side of the river, depriving Neston and Parkgate ports of all their trade.

The Wirral ports obviously objected to the new canal, but when the reclaimed land was drained and turned into agricultural use, there was more agreement. Shipping moved upriver to Chester without being grounded, and small ports, wharves and shipyards sprang up along the new canalized section. For a time it looked like a lasting peace. At last, an answer had been achieved to a problem that had troubled the traders of Chester since Roman times. Kinderley then suggested that a training-wall be continued out to deeper water at Mostyn to arrest the flow and maintain the channel. He also suggested that as much as 7,000 acres of land might be reclaimed by such a project. It was started but never finished.

Thomas Pennant later wrote that the new canalization was destroying the golden beaches of Talacre and Mostyn and they were being silted and grassed-over, as were Neston and Parkgate.

On the English side of the estuary however, businessmen saw an opportunity to improve trade. Robert Stephenson was sought to view plans for the construction of a new canal across the Wirral from Neston to the Manchester Ship canal system. Stephenson put costs in excess of £1 million but the Act was rejected in Parliament on a technicality, probably to do with figures!

In June 1825 a Mr William Chapman looked again at the idea and this time costs were put at £1,560,000. Arguments raged as to the feasibility of such a plan, and it was dropped. In 1826 new plans were submitted to make a deep-water port at Hilbre where the biggest ships of the day might lay-up and a canal be cut to the Mersey at a cost of £1,400,000. Amid charges of duplicity these plans were also dropped. Thomas Telford was consulted regarding the estuary and its silting, and his suggestion mirrored Kindersley's regarding the training wall into deep water. He also suggested that locks be placed across the river so that ships could come and go irrespective of the state of the tides. The answer to the estuary had to be a canal system where the flow could be maintained and controlled. But again there was little enthusiasm for continuing the canal or the training-wall out to Mostyn.

Kinderley's work was soon causing problems. Two bends in the canalized section were causing problems because of erosion and flooding. In 1839 plans were laid to build *groynes* out into the river at a cost of £1,500. A new causeway would cost a further £11,300 and £9,300 was needed for a steam-dredger to maintain a deep channel on this stretch. Meetings to discuss this were hostile and plans were once more shelved.

Trying to maintain the required depth of sixteen-feet in the channel was also proving something of a nightmare. In 1841 plans were laid to remove the weir at Chester (again) to assist the flushing out of the lower river. The Llangollen canal also came under heavy fire for abstracting too much water which was needed in the tidal reaches to assists the scouring out of the river. Both millers and ship-owners on the Dee became very hostile towards the Llangollen canal system's water abstraction.

In the summer of 1841 the Tidal Harbours Committee held an inquiry into the state of the Dee. Serious worries had arisen about the forthcoming plans to lay a railway line along the north Wales coast, and especially its effect on shipping with the poor state of the tidal beats.

On October 17, 1841 the committee went to Chester to see the problem and to take evidence. They discovered that the channel, which was supposed to be sixteen feet, was in fact only eleven feet deep. The main body of the complaint was that the Dee Company had not done anything to assist shipping. There was also serious concern at the proposal by a railway company to build four crossings of the Dee, which would affect shipping and cause more silting.

The Dee Company for its part claimed it had done nothing wrong. The law stated that a depth of sixteen-feet should be maintained on 'a moderate spring tide', the Company's argument being that 'moderate spring tide' had not been defined. The matter was a legal minefield and the matter of maintenance of the channel was allowed to rest.

But in 1849 the then Chester Corporation wrote to the Admiralty supporting earlier reports. They also requested a parliamentary enquiry be held into the state of the river and, in particular, Chester's future as a port.

A team took more evidence in 1850, resulting in 'The Dee Standardisation Restoration Act 1851'. There was some improvement in the channel and ships began to move again. The Dee Company attempted to restore shipping charges, clashing with the Chester Corporation who claimed it would drive trade away. They still claimed that the depth was not being properly maintained. The Corporation threatened legal action and the Dee Company withdrew the charges.

On June 14, 1880 a deputation approached what was by then the Dee Board demanding that Chester weir be demolished so that the estuarine beats could be better flushed, making it easier to maintain a channel of the lawfully required sixteen feet. The Board replied that there were too many Acts governing the river, and that a new single Act was required.

A Mr Henry Robertson again attempted to revive the plans for extending the canal to the lower beats of the river, and to put floodgates in place. This met with great opposition from the ports above Connah's Quay, with claims that all trade would be switched to Mostyn and Connah's Quay, and might not be retrieved. The plans were dropped.

An Act was passed in 1884 allowing the building of a railway crossing over the Dee between Queensferry and Connah's Quay. Known as Hawarden Bridge, on it is a small station known as the Hawarden Bridge

Halt (on the Wrexham / Bidston line). The fifty-year-old groynes at Queensferry were removed when this bridge was built and the training-wall was extended at Fflint. Some work was also done on the embankment. The channel was re-dredged and tolls were reintroduced for the first time since 1819. The total cost of the work was £22,300. An attempt to pass a Dee Conservancy Bill on May 19 1885 failed because of problems with landowners and traders, but the board made a further £4,000 available for the Queensferry Bridge in 1897. The Dee Board however was nearly bankrupt and in 1906 put all the reclaimed land from the canalization up for public auction. Prior to this, it had been rented out for agriculture use.

The last extensive work to be carried out on the upper section of the estuarine area of the river was in 1890, apart from embankment erosion to prevent flooding. Periodic dredging still took place near shipyards, but Chester port was dying. Today the river is still dredged up to Connah's Quay for the wharf at Summers Jetty (British Steel). Ships can no longer go higher than Queensferry because of the road-bridges. Only small boats, mostly fishing and privately owned pleasure craft, go higher these days.

Kinderley was under instructions that when he canalized the river he must protect the two recognised crossings, both of which were to be protected by law. The crossing at Saltney was known as Higher Ferry and the one at Queensferry (then Kingsferry) known as Lower Ferry. These names could still be seen on the destination boards of the local Crosville buses until the 1960's, when bridges had long replaced the ferries.

The law provided that a rowing boat be available day and night at the Higher Ferry crossing, with a person being responsible for its maintenance and operation. A salmon fisherman from the Mersey named Manifold, who was employed on building a nearby farmhouse, was employed. A small farmhouse on the banks at the crossing point came with the job, and the Manifold family stayed until the ferry was replaced by a foot-bridge.

Lower Ferry was a very different affair. Situated where the Old Ferry Bridge stands today, a large flat-bottomed boat of a windlass type was used to carry people and livestock across the Dee. A two-man crew manned it and they made a brisk trade. In 1897 a bridge replaced the boat, and was opened by Gladstone. The small single-span bridge that Gladstone opened soon proved insufficient for the needs of the industry that was sprouting-up all along Deeside and the Wirral. In 1926 a new hydraulic bridge that opened to allow ships through replaced it. This is the bridge that is known as the 'Old Ferry Bridge'. The electric motors that operated the drawbridge have been removed. There is an excellent footbridge across it from which can be seen the remains of the supporting walls from the original single-track bridge alongside.

In the summer of 1951, a traffic jam stretched from Queensferry to Prestatyn. It was obvious that the two-lanes of the Old Ferry Bridge could not accommodate the vast increase in traffic, so out came the slide-rules and pens and a third bridge – a metal box-bridge that could not be opened – was built, along with the Queensferry by-pass. Opened in 1962 at a cost of £241,857 it not only signalled an end to traffic jams but also an end to shipping above Summers Steelworks at Shotton.

The Old Ferry Bridge underwent a major repaint and some repair during 1990. The wooden supports that covered the bridge stanchions were removed leaving the bridge looking ugly and naked, even with its new coat of paint. The wood was fitted in the days when sailing ships still travelled to Chester and the smaller ports, the reason being that should the ship collide with the stanchion, then the impact of wood on wood might be less damaging than wood on metal. Apparently such collisions were not unusual as the ships struggled to find the channel.

Years ago, one could see the bones of an old ship, partially submerged in the silt just downstream of the ferry bridge. These were in fact the remains òf the old windlass ferry that was replaced by the Gladstone bridge in 1897. The ferry was grounded, all her brass and steering gear having been removed. She was left to lie on the silt, slowly sinking.

Having gone there to photograph her one sunny Sunday morning, I was bitterly disappointed to find that she had gone. An elderly gentleman who lived nearby was amused to inform me that it was he who had removed the bones by sawing them for firewood. I was not amused but there it was. If it was so important, he asked why didn't the council remove it and restore it years ago? It was a valid question and asked by many people.

Bob Manifold, the last man to row passengers across the Dee at the higher ferry crossing, now uses his old rowing boat for salmon fishing, having been given it by Flintshire County Council on his retirement. He also relates a very interesting story about a depression in a field close to the Chester – Sealand – Queensferry road.

This, he said, is where a ship foundered in a severe gale sometime before 1740. There was a great loss of life, mostly Welshmen, and some bodies were never recovered because of the silt. Many of the bodies that were found were buried at Sealand. Following the canalization of the river, it was decided that the river's path would form the new boundary between Wales and England. This however caused an argument as it meant that the Welsh sailors who died with that ship would lie in English soil. For this reason, it was decided that the Sealand area should remain in Wales for the sake of the dead sailors.

The field has now been marked lest there be any developments proposed there in the future. The estimated cost of a dig to verify the story is, however, in excess of £1 million.

The third Dee crossing was finished in 1998. An impressive bridge stands where the old Connah's Quay power station once was, linking the A548 with the Wirral. This will ease the traffic flow at Queensferry.

The higher ferry crossing is now a narrow-footbridge that can be reached from the A548 Chester – Sealand road down an unclassified lane. It can be reached from the other side of the river from Saltney, by turning off at Mold Junction.

# The Industrial Development of Deeside

Until the canalization of the Dee employment between Chester and Talacre was mostly related to agriculture and the sea. With the change in the river small ports and wharves sprang-up along the new canalled length and the Dee's potential as a major exporting river became a reality.

### Coal Mining

The potential of coal as a heating fuel and source of energy was only fully exploited during the industrial revolution.

The area was ideally situated to exploit Ireland's lack of this particular brand of 'black stuff', and a vast amount of coal was exported there. It was also part of an important iron, steel, copper and lead producing area, all of which were extremely hungry for coal. Coal was also exported from Connah's Quay to Cornwall, another coal less area where it was needed to fuel the steam engines, this being the return journey for ships that brought china clay to Runcorn. In its latter decades, the area's coal industry was also supplying vast amounts to coal burning power stations such as Connah's Quay and Fiddlers Ferry in Lancashire.

Pony-borne panniers or baskets had been used to transport coal to the ports at Queensferry and Saltney, where it was loaded onto ships. With the developments of the industrial revolution, the panniers were replaced by a small horse-drawn tramway that ran from Aston to Queensferry. Another was later laid to the Sandycroft area.

The north Wales coal field lies in pockets from Point of Air in the west to Saltney Marsh in the east and the area around Wrexham in the south-east. It also contains pockets around Mold. The area of coal over the Dee around Neston is also part of the north Wales coal field, as is the area of coal in Lancashire. The Dee area from Point of Air eastwards was a myriad of small private pits during the 17th, 18th and 19th century, many of which today are under housing estates, roads, factories, airfields and all manner of developments. Three hundred and twenty mines have been counted in Mostyn alone, one hundred of these having names.

Coal was probably mined on Mostyn land as early as 1294, this probably being the earliest exploited area. The Mostyns had a considerable advantage in owning their own port, ships being the only means of moving a considerable tonnage of any material until the industrial revolution. A new pit was sunk in Mostyn in the 1630's to exploit a rich new seam, which was affected by a common problem in coalmines. *Firedamp* has caused explosions and deaths in coalmines throughout the history of the industry. It consists of methane or carburetted hydrogen that is produced from decaying vegetable matter, and problems arise when this combines with air, being combustible at certain ratios. The new pit had halted work because there was methane present, and during attempts to restart work a huge explosion occurred some fifty feet below ground on February 3, 1675.

The then owner, Sir Roger Mostyn (he of the Civil War) wrote an explicit account of the explosion in which he also described several heroic attempts by himself to save the lives of his workers. The pit had been closed for three days before the steward thought it might be safe to go underground. The men, according to Mostyn, wanted to go with him and one had a lighted candle. Whether this was the case, or whether the combination became self-combustible, there was an explosion that was heard fifteen miles away. Men were thrown through the air, one of them over trees at the pit head, six perished and others were very severely injured. The horse-whimsey at the pit head was also apparently destroyed.

Many Welsh collieries suffered major disasters at some time or other in their working life. It must be remembered that when Mostyn referred to 'men', these possibly included boys of as young as ten years, and also possibly women. Many mansions in Wales were built from money made through mining, the owners making enormous profits while the people who created the wealth died early through working long hours in some of the unhealthiest circumstances probably known to man.

Coal mining at Mostyn came to an end in 1884, the tunnels flooding when water poured through the walls from previous workings. Pit ponies were drowned and, although no human lives were lost, the community was decimated by three hundred people losing their work. They had no other calling and the disaster caused many families to move away in search of a living.

Another medieval mining area was to be found around Ewloe. There was here a fascinating punishment attached to the common practise of stealing coal. Its name was the *law of Hopedale*, and it offered the offender a medieval version of three chances and out. The first two occasions that a man was caught stealing coal, he was given warnings. The third time, however, he was taken underground and pinned to pit props by means of strategically placed daggers through the hands. He would then be left to his own devices. Should he manage to free himself, the matter was over. Should he fail to free himself, he died!

The other area to have very early coal workings was Talacre, which included Picton Pool from where Jasper Tudor is reputed to have sailed for France having escaped from Mostyn Hall. This area also had the last working coal mine in north Wales.

Point of Air closed in 1996 having been taken over from the Coal Board by R J Budge (RJB Mining) in 1994. At that time there were six miles of tunnel under the sea and the coal face was some two and a half miles from the coast. The two shafts leading to these tunnels were nearly a thousand metres deep each. Pit ponies were still in use at Point of Air as lately as the 1970's. Once underground, the ponies never saw daylight until they retired. The miners held these brave little workers in great affection, taking enormous pride in their appearance and welfare. The Miners Strike of 1984 split Point of Air, causing continuous controversy and incessant backbiting within a community half of which worked and half of which striked. When RJB came up with its ultimate geological report, there was, and still is, twenty million tons of coal waiting to be cut at Point of Air. Most of the people who worked there, especially in the stressful conditions after 1984, would rather it stay there.

## Lead Mining

The Romans mined lead from the rich seams that ran through the Pentre Halkyn and Holywell areas although no trace has been found of their mines, probably because they were incorporated into later workings.

The Grosvenors of Eaton Hall had considerable mining interests in Flintshire and Denbighshire in the 16th and 17th centuries, and in 1692 the London Lead Company began to mine extensively in this part of north Wales. They left in 1786 to concentrate on mining interests in Cumbria. By the 18th century however, a chain of lead works were set up along the Dee estuary taking advantage of the power of water from wells and streams, of heat from coal and of transport on the estuary. Official statistics show that between 1845 and 1938, 657,000 tons of lead was mined and 341,601 tons of zinc, equivalent to 13% of the total production of Britain. The highest output was during the 1850's – 60's, after which there was a sharp decline that deepened considerably after 1910. Two thousand seven hundred and eighty-six lead mines were recorded in 1851, but just six hundred and sixty-four remained by 1911.

Halkyn District United Lead Mines was formed in 1928 from a number of smaller units. The company extended the levels, creating new tunnelling world records in the process. Work was suspended over World War II but operations resumed after hostilities ended.

The London Lead Company had a coal powered smelting furnace at Gadlys, Holywell from 1703, where silver was also refined. Llanerch-y-Mor had its own smelting works from the mid 18th century, and this closed in 1900. Lead was smelted in a single furnace known as a *bale* and this survives today in place names such as Pen-y-Bâl (Holywell).

The biggest evidence of lead mining in north Wales today however are the scars from spoil-tips and concern over toxic run-offs from flooded pits into waterways. The extent of lead mining over the centuries, and the ignorance of people to the toxicity of the element, is still causing headaches for conservationists who worry about waste and discharges in such highly populated and environmentally sensitive areas.

## Iron and Steel Works

The Mostyn Ironworks was the first plant on Deeside, built on the side of Mostyn Docks and largely self-contained. John Summers came to Deeside in 1896 and bought 200 acres of reclaimed land alongside the Dee at Shotton, and began to build his iron-works. It is said that he paid one shilling per acre for the site and was attracted to the area because of the availability of labour, a good railway system and a navigable river.

Shotton was producing 600 tons of sheets within days of the factory opening. It had ten open-hearth furnaces. In 1910 Garden City was built to cater for the increased work force that was required from inland Denbighshire, Merseyside, Flintshire and Cheshire. At its height the factory employed 13,000 people. Pig iron came up the Dee and iron ore from Bidston docks directly into the works by rail. They had their own fleet of ships and their own railway locomotives named after the planets.

By 1950 6,000 workers were employed and it became obvious that the number would be insufficient for the needs of steel in the boom-years after the war. They were then producing over 7,000 tons of steel per week and the trend was up. It was in the 1950's that the management of both

Summers and Courtauld's made their famous speeches that they would provide work for generation after generation on Deeside. Geoffrey Summers suggested that there should be one council body to govern the whole of industrial Deeside. The council acquired Red Hall Estate in Connah's Quay and Aston Estate was still growing on Aston Hill. Other industries were also growing and demand for housing was continuous. The council planned to build over a thousand homes for the work force of Deeside.

The boom lasted only until the 1970's. Courtauld's closed and Summers steelworks chopped its workforce from 13,000 to just 2,000. Deeside looked like a ghost town with haulage, coal and other related industries being thrown onto a slag heap of over 20,000 workers. There had been the boom – now it was time for bust. Today, following the massive closure programme, Shotton survives as British Steel employing just 2,000 people. It is a rolling mill and has recently spent £75 million on more up to date rolling equipment.

## Other related Industries on Deeside

### Textiles

Llangollen had several mills, the most important of which was Lower Dee Mills, opened in 1805 by two Manchester men, William Turner and Andrew Comber.

Lower Mills span and weaved. It was totally rebuilt and modernised in 1815, but burnt down in 1819 and the owners went bankrupt. The mill lay idle until 1824 when another Manchester owner came along, but he too went bankrupt in the great slump of 1830. It was then converted to produce flannel and woollen cloth, continuing until 1967. Upper Dee Mills produced cloth from 1855 until its closure in 1920.

Cotton spinning came to Holywell in 1777 with John Smalley who later went into partnership with John Chambers. The company survived the slump of 1837 but went into liquidation in 1841. Courtauld's later came to Fflint and Greenfield. At their height they employed over 7,000 workers, but they folded in the 1970's.

*   *   *

Alyn & Deeside Council is proud that, following the redundancies at Shotton and the closure of Courtauld's on Deeside, more than three quarters of the job losses have been replaced by modern industrial developments.

Deeside has certainly done more than its share to ensure that employment remains high, especially compared with many other Welsh regions. The new power station at Connah's Quay, the oil and gas terminals near Talacre and the prospect of an enlarged Mostyn Docks complex point towards further employment prospects, and most of the required skills are already available in the area.

Shotton paper is the biggest maker of printing and high-class paper in the UK and their biggest plant is now erected on the Deeside Industrial Estate on part of what was the former Sealand air-field. Iceland Foods and Toyota Car Engines are also there, along with a book-full of other employers.

Apart from a readily available pool of skilled employees waiting to pull on overalls, the most praised attraction is the close proximity of the railway system. The London-Holyhead main line runs through Deeside, passing also through Crewe and other crucial interchanges. There is also an excellent local network of motorways that is linked to the national motorway system giving access to the big ports of Liverpool and Birkenhead, or to the east coast ports of England for Europe. It is ironic that the port of Birkenhead, which helped kill off the small ports on the river Dee, has been given a new lease of life by new industries of Deeside, some built on land that was once part of the now dead Dee ports.

Because of the excellent communication lines, goods can be at ports within hours of being completed and clients can be at meetings in Deeside within an hour of landing at Manchester Airport. Forty-four ton articulated lorries are better acquainted with large motorways than country lanes, giving Deeside an enormous advantage over many other areas of northeastern Wales.

Nathaniel Kinderley, a far-sighted unsung hero of the 18th century has much to be thanked for. Although the river no longer plays any part in the transportation plans of the big companies, without its canalization, all that is happening here today would have been impossible. He had distractors during and after his time,but much of what has been done since the 1740s has been to do with flood prevention. It might be said therefore that Nathaniel Kinderley put Deeside on the map.

# Piracy and Smuggling on the River Dee

Much of the north Wales coastline is a myriad of sandy coves and small river mouths, many of which can take a small boat on a full tide. A sparse population made it ideal country for smuggling, and there was a strong tradition of smugglers from the island of Anglesey to the island of Hilbre. Provided that the boatmen knew the channels and sandbanks it was a way of making a good living, even if it was not a good way of making a living.

From the late 1400s the *Creek of Chester* became known as a major smuggling area where almost anything could be bought – at a price. Watergate Street today is a pleasant street, but it used to be full of seedy warehouses and dark alleys where loose women plied their trade and evil-minded men lay in wait for merchants making their way to the docks, heavy with drink. Silver and gold buttons, felt and fur hats, and expensively trimmed clothes were the quarry, as well as purses stuffed with coins. It was not a place to be after dark!

In 1586 one Julian Maignaire came to Chester seeking goods he had been robbed of whilst his ship was at sea. His ship, the *Golden Falcon*, was en-route from St Malo to Flushing but he had been informed that the goods lay in a Watergate Street warehouse in Chester. He petitioned the Mayor for a warrant to search the premises, resulting in the discovery of the stolen goods.

A Chester ship *Elizabeth of Gayton* operated by one Richard Johnson was attacked in 1656 by pirates whilst *en-route* from Holyhead to Chester. The pirates demanded a ransom of £30 for the Captain, which was paid. In 1562 a ship called *The James* was set upon by pirates in the estuary after she had left Chester port. Her cargo of fine linen and wines were all taken. In 1585 an enquiry was held into a ship that was raided whilst in port at Chester. The pirates are thought to have been Spaniards, the ship being French. During the fighting one crewman was killed and tossed into the river Dee. The Mayor of Chester was besieged with complaints by shipowners as late as 1761, and for action to be taken against pirates in the estuary. During the Napoleonic wars the trade between Chester and Ireland suffered badly because of French ships waiting off the Dee estuary and seizing what they could of cargo and ships.

Naval ships also visited Chester in the old days, bringing in their wake the dreaded press-gangs. These volunteered people into a career in the armed forces by the persuasive use of a tap from a truncheon. Many awoke on one of HM ships, way out at sea, fully enlisted in the navy. It was common for men seeking female company to wander the darkened streets of the dock area, finding a suitable woman to engage in conversation, and knowing nothing more about it until they awoke on a ship out at sea. The lady of the night received no money from her potential client but was more than recompensed by the press-gangs.

Another connection with slavery was the trade in human cargo through the city. The Dixon family of Chester was involved in slave trading during the 18th century. They were ship-owners who were very prominent in opposing the ending of the slave trade. Ormerod's *History of Cheshire* (1882) records that from Saxon times the port of Chester was famous for its trade in horses of fine quality as well as in slaves, mostly from abroad. There is little by way of documentation about the slave trade from the Dee however, but it was known to be considerable. In 1756 a ship called the *Black Prince* out of Chester was attacked, along with two Liverpool ships, off Melumbra, West Africa. All three ships were slave-traders and were destroyed by the French navy.

Mostyn and some of the smaller wharves in that area were particularly involved in smuggling. Luxury goods that incurred heavy taxation, including tobacco, linen, wines and salt, were the most often smuggled commodities. Since the trade was controlled by 'high up' people, very little is recorded because of a distinct lack of prosecuting – the people who benefited the most from smuggled luxury goods were also the people who sat in judgement over transgressors.

Today's smuggling on the coastline of north Wales is nothing new, but the modern trade is mostly in drugs. The most recent method is to drop the drugs at given locations in waterproof containers that sink to the sea-bed, to be recovered later. The trade was highlighted when fishing trawlers lifted considerable amounts of drugs in their nets. The drugs are dropped from planes or ships. It is a deadly business that greatly concerns the police, and their helicopter is fitted with accurate technical equipment to help detect such illegal work.

# The Last Ferryman

Following the canalization of the Dee from Saltney to Fflint, which straightened and deepened the river, boats replaced the ancient fords. Lower Ferry (at Queensferry) became a windlass operated flat-bottomed boat capable of taking livestock and carriages. A bridge replaced it only in 1897. The Higher Ferry crossing is unusual inasmuch as just one family maintained the rowing boat across it from its instigation until its replacing by a bridge.

In 1740 the authorities were looking for someone to operate the rowing boat crossing and a man was found nearby. He was a salmon fisherman from the Mersey by the name of Manifold, who was then employed on the construction of a farmhouse in the Saughall area. He took the job of ferryman and, according to his descendants, Manifolds were the official ferrymen until a bridge was erected in the late 1960s. The Manifolds lasted a staggering two hundred and twenty-eight years. It all came to an end when stunned staff from the then Flintshire County Council called and discovered that the ferryboat was still operational. They first replaced the rowlocks and oars with an outboard, and later with a footbridge.

It was on a sunny May day that I approached a delightful cottage overlooking the Dee in search of an interview. A well-built gentleman of medium height opened the door. He had large tanned hands and arms, and a ruddy complexion. Obviously this was the son so I enquired as to the whereabouts of Mr Bob Manifold, the last ferryman on the Dee. He laughed, asked me inside, and quietly explained that this was a common reaction, but he was in fact 86 years old. The following is taken from the interview that occurred on May 19, 1985.

\* \* \*

This cottage stands where the original ferryman's farmhouse was built. The Saltney marshes had some fearsome villagers then who raided anyone who passed on a horse. Oh yes those stories are true, but a little before my time – it happened during the 1700s.

My first memories of the Dee are being with my father when I was a lad. The Dee was much busier then of course, and it was all fast sleek schooners being taken up or down in-tow, and we had to be careful of them on the ferry. I could lie in bed here and listen to them creak and groan as they passed by, perhaps laden with goods for some foreign shore. They were splendid to see with white sails aloft and they were very fast and low in the water. I remember the iron-ore schooners coming upstream, laden and very low in the water. They headed for Saltney wharf or Brymbo steelworks, as many as six at a time in-tow behind a tugboat.

The tugboats were a pickle at times. The schooners came in to the bar and stood-off, waiting for a tow. If the tide was a low one they came up as far as they could and waited at one of the ports. The tugs were always late and there was hell to play because finding a berth in the ports wasn't easy. Having arrived at the schooner, the tug would circle her and demand a fee to take her in-tow. It was the company that refused to pay for a tow and the schooner captain was often left to sort matters out, at his own expense. The fees were often far too high, and perishable cargoes rotted as the arguments raged and the tide fell away. There were some tiresome tugboat captains who lined their own pockets but, with the Dee being as she was, the sail-ships were at the mercy of the tugboat captains and their demands.

Schooners had to be light and low to be fast. Our Dee schooners were around the one hundred and sixty-ton mark, with hand-carved fittings everywhere and cabins like church-pews, covered in carvings. Being low they flooded easily on a slight sea let alone a rough one, and there was always a problem with men being washed over-board, some never to be seen again. Some of the bigger schooners were later fitted with an auxiliary engine which was helpful when they were becalmed out at sea, or if there was insufficient wind to enter or leave a port.

My Uncle Johnny had a schooner - all sail and very fast. They could handle well on a rough sea, especially if the captain knew his stuff. They would respond like a dream in the proper hands, no matter how bad the weather. And some of the fastest and finest schooners were built here on the Dee by Ferguson & Baird. Uncle Johnny took his wife everywhere on his schooner, and they were happy. But some didn't like their wives on board - it was obvious why because they tramped port to port.

My memories of Chester Port are not that impressive really. Chester's heyday was before my time, although I remember ships leaving there with cheese for all over the world. It was Saltney wharf that was busy up there. I remember coal and all manner of cargoes coming and going to Saltney. But you know, people forget just how important the canals were in Cheshire to the ports. Chester had a terminal for barges that fed the ships in port, near where Crosville is today. The seaports relied heavily on those canals and they served them well. I can remember Chester canal being so busy it was jammed at times. People think today of the canals being just for pleasure boating, but in their hey-day there was no time for pleasure bcause those canals were vital to the Chester port.

Saltney was busier than Connah's Quay in its time. A heck of a lot of coal went through there, brought in by ship and on to Brymbo steelworks by train. And remember, those sidings were directly linked to the main Holyhead – London line, so anywhere could be reached. Every power station and steelwork wanted coal at that time.'

The most famous tugboat on the river was the *Manxman* out of Connah's Quay. She was a steamer, taking ships in-tow from the ports, or picking them up at Wild Roads (an area off Talacre) or from the Prestatyn gutter.

She was a normal sized tugboat, the same as those on the Mersey and very powerful. She could face all weathers and was much in demand. The tugs saved the ship-owners a lot of money by their speed in getting ships in or away. The railway company brought their own tugs in, and started a price war. Tugging was profitable so some did it for nothing, just to keep the railway boats away because they always demanded a charge. All the estuaries were the same and all captains were under the same pressure with cargoes. You must remember that there were many bad slumps on the Welsh coast and many ships were laid-up at anchor for weeks. Some never got to sea again.

We never did much with the explosives from Queensferry if we could help it. Any ship loading there had to show a red flag and everyone got away from her as fast as possible. That was a very busy port because after the explosives they sent huge loads of tar from there.

Point of Air Colliery docks had a funny lot up there. They had their own boats and kept themselves to themselves very much. Coppacks of Connah's Quay did a bit for them and I remember a ship catching fire as she left the port, and she sank there (*Santa Rosa*).

During the First World War the *Earl of Latham*, a Dee ship, was sunk off Ireland by the Germans in 1915. She was running with the *Kathleen & Mary*, another Coppack ship out of the Quay. They were in thick fog off Ireland with the *Earl of Latham* in front. She was shelled by the Germans and lost, but the *Kathleen & Mary* got away in the fog. When the German U-boat captain realised that she was a harmless freighter, he came on deck and shot himself. People said that it was the *Lusitainia* they were after, and in the fog the *Earl* looked bigger than she was.

Mind you, some schooners were fitted with cannon on their decks. The plan was simple: when the Germans stopped firing the crews slipped over the side in full view, leaving the gunners hidden onboard. The crews got away in rowboats. The unsuspecting U-boats were then relaxed and ready to be taken by the gunners on board. That caused them some problems I can tell you. A favourite place for this was the mouth of the Dee, where they lay in wait for ships from the Dee and the Mersey; but many were damaged and some sunk by schooners.

Between the wars there was very little activity really because trade was slipping away to Liverpool by then, except for the Quay and Mostyn. There was some flat-bottomed boat traffic, but the smaller ports began to rust away a bit. We had some bad winters on the Dee, I can tell you. Schooners went past here in-tow, all iced-up, and the crews working like fury to clean them. Remember, those ships had no cover on the steering wheel. If you were out in a heavy freezing sea, you froze in what you wore. I often stood out in a Force Eight gale, frozen stiff, and you had a cup of cocoa at midnight if you were lucky. If your clothes were wet when you took them off, then they were wet again when you put them on for the next shift. And some ships were lost through icing-up alone, they were so low in the water.

*Bob laughed loudly when asked about smuggling on the Dee.* Yes. But there's a rule that the less you see. the better it is. Frankly you just don't want to bother. Yes there is smuggling; there always has been and there always will be. But it's best to keep clear and know nothing.

Now that the axe has fallen and the ferry is finished, I feel sad, very sad indeed. It was in our family for two hundred and twenty or more, and always with a rowing boat. I loved the work, and the people. But one day a fella came here from the council and watched me rowing people to and fro across the river. He didn't even know that my job existed. I told him how proud we Manifolds were of the ferry, and of the relationship we had with the people. He insisted that my oars be replaced by an outboard engine and I refused. But he insisted and one came, and I had to use the damn thing.

Then another fella come from the council and said that the ferry was to be replaced by a bridge, and that was final. I tried to tell him we didn't need one. I told him about the history of the ferry, but the damn bridge came. I told them I wasn't giving in and I went salmon fishing. There was no way that I was leaving the river – not after over two hundred years.

If them fellas from the council hadn't come here interfering, the ferry would have run another two hundred years. The people loved it, so why change it? I worked all hours, whenever I was wanted. There was the railway at Saltney – big in the 1940's-50's, and the airfields. They came and knocked me up at five in the morning, and sometimes earlier if there was overtime money on offer, and out I went. It was difficult in rough weather with big tides, but most of them were regulars I knew them well and we shared many a laugh.

One fella came on a freezing winter's morning with a bike. We got into the boat and I started to row across. He was tired and leant on his bike and fell asleep, and he fell into the river. It was hell trying to get him back into the boat because he was all tied-up with his bike.

In those days the local police were always the same ones, and everybody knew everybody very well. They'd call here and ask me to keep a lookout for bodies or missing persons. We always worked very well together.

One day a young policeman called reporting that a young girl was missing and wanted to kill herself. I said I'd do my best to find her for him. Later that day I found her in the river and she was very violent, she wanted to die and did her best to take me along with her, but I wanted to live and to save her. I got her into the boat and took her home, and was pleased I'd done my bit. Later, the police called and said she'd killed herself another way and that upset me very badly indeed, she was so young.

On another day I had a young policeman with me and we were looking for a body this time. I knew where she'd be and off we went. I expected the tide to fetch her-up in the bushes below the cottage here and there she was.

It was not amusing, though I can laugh about it now: the bobby hadn't seen a body before and once I felt her and said that she was dead. He went pale. While we were trying to get her on board he was sick and I was left to get the body on board, and at the same time stop the policeman from falling into the river whilst being sick. It was a hell of a day that one I can tell you. But, I managed.

My working day was usually from five in the morning till ten at night, or later in summer. Often I had to row coffins and mourners across and keeping an upset family straight on rough water was no picnic – the only ones that never complained were them in the box.

In the Second War it was funny. Total strangers would often hail me by shouting out 'Ferry' and I'd go to them. There were many shady chaps in long coats that never said a dickey all the way across the river, and then just jumped out and went away in the night. I'd go cold as I rowed them and God only knew who they were. It was always best to be quiet and say nothing to them, we were always warned by the police about *fifth columnists*.

When Broughton airfield was at its height and the massive railway yards at Mold Junction (Saltney) were in full use, the ferry was busy, many travelling on cycles from the Chester – Saughall areas to work in the industries. Being a remote area, the ferry was also much used by unsavoury black-market characters. They didn't say much and what their mission was I never bothered to ask. But I rowed like hell to reach the other side just to get shut of them .

Crossing in the ferry watching those old sailboats coming and going was a special kind of magic that I really miss very much. They grounded easily off Connah's Quay and it was a work of art to bring them in sometimes, depending on how the river was running. Those sandbanks out there are dangerous and I've rescued many a man cockling off Fflint or the Quay. All I'd see as I rowed out to net off Hilbre was a hand sticking above the silts. If I were lucky I'd get them on board and on to dry land. I never asked who they were even, just shook a muddy hand and was away again. But there were many that were unable to tell me who they were – they were dead.

I've never bothered about cockles myself and I worry about the new super-breed of cockler out there, now they've come back, from dawn till dusk. Half of them don't know the beds of the estuary at all. It's so dangerous.

Now, the Dee tidal-bore was fun. People came from miles around to see it and often asked would I take them to 'ride-it' in my boat. I'd row down the river and a good bore comes upstream in excess of 30mph in rough weather. The front-end of the boat hit the bore and went up in the air, and everybody laughed or screamed. They got very wet but they loved it and knew they were safe with me.

One day there was quite a strange chap on board who'd said nothing downstream but got excited as the bore approached. Suddenly I knew that he wanted to kill himself and, as he jumped, I threw myself at him and tried to hold the boat straight and get the other to hang onto him We did it, but it spoilt the trip.

I came out one morning just before five in the morning and there was this chap on the opposite bank running up and down, shouting. His daughter had been missing since one o'clock and he feared the worst. I knew the tide was up at two o'clock and, if she had gone in, I knew where she'd be. I took him so far, then sent him off for the police.

Sadly, she was there floating and thick with mud and slime. The bobby who came seemed lively enough. 'We'd better wash her down a bit I think.' I said and asked the policeman to help. This was his first body and he froze in fear on the bank and couldn't move, so I did it. But he was a nice lad afterwards and we did much to help each other.

Wynford Vaughan-Thomas asked me how I felt cutting my place in history. It was a job handed to me from my father, and from his father and so on. If that darn bridge wasn't there now, I'd not have time to talk to you as I'd be crossing folk in my boat. The council said it was progress but since that bridge went up we've had nothing but trouble. Youths with motor cycles, drunks and people being dropped off from cars at all hours and scurrying away carrying goodness knows what.

Do you know, they gave me a clock dated June 17, 1968 to commemorate the new bridge. The council thought I'd go quietly into hiding. They let me keep the boat, and I joined my son netting for salmon. But watching the bridge being constructed, I wanted to pull it down bit by bit because of the history it was replacing and the joy and sorrow that crossing had brought me. I knew on that last trip on that last day, that a way of life would be going that could have lasted another two hundred years. All that fool from the council talked of was 'progress'. What did he ever know about the ferry as a way of life?

No more funerals come across or tired cyclists fall into the water. I wouldn't have swapped a day of this life on the ferry for anything or anyone.

\* \* \*

*Bob Manifold died not long after. There was much more to ask, and it was his son, Peter Manifold, who filled in the gaps on this remarkable story.*

\* \* \*

I took much of the ferrying duties between 1959 and 1961 because my father was away fishing on the estuary. I remember very early one morning faintly seeing the shape of a cyclist approaching the ferry at great speed, and hailing me from a crossing.

I rowed towards the cyclist, with my back to him of course, but when I got there, the cyclist had gone. Looking around, I saw a cap in the water and the cyclist emerged, blowing water out of his mouth like a fountain. The young man was something of a tear-away on his cycle and his 'mates' had put engine grease on the rims at his place of work. He couldn't stop at the ferry and somersaulted right into the freezing Dee. Thank God, he saw the funny side of it, even while the twisted cycle frame was still about his neck.

When war broke out in 1939 my father built his own *Anderson* style air-raid shelter. It was a deep hole supported on all sides with railway sleepers, and an old boat upturned for a roof, strengthened by metal and a bank of soil. It was the best shelter in the country. One day us lads were on the river embankment watching a dogfight over Broughton airfield, just across the river from the cottage. We were shouting and jeering but, when I looked at the river, there was Dad in his boat, shouting abuse at us to get into the shelter in language I'd not heard before. How he never tippled that boat over I'll never know. The German plane was shot down and landed in the field at the rear of our home, and the crew was arrested by the Home Guard. It was all very exciting and in the heat Dad forgot to deal with us for ignoring the well-rehearsed air-raid drill.

One day we saw a fighter air-craft trying to get back to Broughton airfield and it was seriously crippled from enemy attack. On the way down it clipped the top of a tree and began to descend to the river. In a flash, Dad was in that boat and rowing like fury downstream towards the plane. We watched it all and just as he arrived at the plane it sank. Dad dived into the river and managed to free the cockpit cover and get the pilot out, but sadly he was dead when Dad got him to the bank. It was a marvellous effort and one that few people ever heard about. He was ill over that incident. So young a man to die within yards of the airfield and help.

Another day I saw a bomber coming in to Broughton with engines feathering. The crew bailed out and landed in the Dee. One of the farm workers ran to assist and when he arrived at the riverbank, he was so breathless that he couldn't tell the crew to get out of the harness quickly because of the tide. I think they were foreigners and we watched as the current pulled them and their chutes down to a watery grave. It was like a slow-motion film watching it, and there was nothing we could do.

But an amusing incident was when a fighter aircraft nose-dived into the silt on the riverside. The Ministry came and removed most of it, but left a lot in the silt. Dad took off in the boat and we helped him to remove the cockpit-canopy which we later made into a draining board for the cottage. That wreck is still there today and sometimes shows on low water.

Another time my brother and I were with Dad going downstream in the boat when we saw a hat floating. All items of clothing are inspected as a matter of course because so often there is someone attached to them. This was no different and under the hat was a woman trying to kill herself. She went mad trying to get Dad and us lads in with her. She was big and strong and she pulled the boat almost over. In the current we went off towards Queensferry. As we approached, there were a couple of bobbies on the road bridge and we shouted for assistance. Obviously they thought we were fishing or fooling and they waved back laughing 'Hi Bob, nice day'. Thankfully, just in time they got the measure of things and came to help. Somehow we got her ashore alive and still fighting and we were all so knackered that the fishing trip was ruined. But the crowning glory of it all was, as the policemen came nearer, a huge woman from the cottage by the bridge who was the sister of our victim came yelling and screaming down the bank at us. She ran into the river, and blow me if she didn't collapse as well so we had to drag both of them out. It was a nightmare.

But it wasn't all gloom and doom on the Saltney Ferry. It had its lighter moments, like the gentlemen in pinstriped suits who were supervising a property rebuild nearby. They enquired about the tidal-bore and when Dad explained, they wanted to ride it in Dad's boat. It was a recipe for disaster. Off they went in pinstripes and bowlers and Dad rowed for the bore. Up went the boat and the water gushed in. All that afternoon the hedge opposite the cottage was covered in pinstriped suits drying in the sunshine, with very disgruntled gentlemen sitting on the bank in their under-wear. It was one of the best laughs of my life.

The local Home Guard trained in the fields and woodlands in the Saltney and Saughall area in the War and Dad was a leader. He gave instructions to the men on how to use a rowing-boat and instructions on current and tides, etc. There was a camp of Royal Engineers nearby and their instructor was quite impressed by Dad's ability to train the men.

Dad was very pleased when they asked him to undertake the business of training the men in rowing. He was strict on discipline and the men responded. But lying in bed at night was frightful, because all I could hear was Dad on the river with the men, shouting 'In, Out, In, Out'. It drove us crackers.

Then one day they wanted to build a pontoon bridge across the Dee, as an exercise. It was finished just on dusk. The following morning the Engineers officer screaming and shouting and looking out of the cottage window awaked us. Dad was doubled-up laughing because the bridge had gone – washed away on the tide. Dad had told them, but they knew better. That kept us all laughing throughout the war.

But Dad did take his Home Guard seriously. One night they planned an attack on a local isolated public house, the object of the exercise being to free the British prisoners inside it from the Germans. It was planned to the last detail except that nobody told the licensee.

About two in the morning, all hell let loose inside and outside the pub with guns and ammunition being fired, real and dummy. Someone called the police and there were lengthy explanations for some time afterwards.

Dad was very badly affected by the closure of the ferry. After all the handshakers and suits went back to their offices, they came and took his ferry-boat away. I know he told you different, but it was taken away and sold for probably a few quid. He'd looked after it like it was his own. Flintshire County Council treated him badly after all those years of ferrying – the family did it for over two hundred years. They broke his heart, because the public wanted him to stay as ferryman. To be honest, it could have stayed that way for his lifetime then perhaps a change would have been more acceptable. They didn't know or care how he felt.

*   *   *

# Captain Joe Fellows – A Man of Sail

I visited the hut that was built for 'The Quay Watermans Association' on part of the old Connah's Quay docks in the summer of 1985 and asked some elderly gentlemen whether there were any of the old Quay sea captains still alive. Captain Joe they all said – ninety-two years of age, and just the man. As I asked about the state of his health, one of the party said 'Here he comes now, just in time for you'.

I stared disbelievingly as a sprightly man, small of stature and well dressed, strode towards the hut. There were cries of 'Morning Joe' and an offer of a seat. This could not be a man in his nineties, I thought. One of the men explained the situation to the Captain, and he said 'Let me finish these fish and chips and we'll go back to my house up the village'.

* * *

The secret to keeping young is a lean diet, no ale and plenty of hard work. I don't drink, but I am a regular visitor to the local club. I tell them stories of the days of sail out of Connah's Quay docks.

My first memories of the sea were from about 1910. I went as cook on a schooner, the *Margaret Hobley* out of Llanelli. Captain John Hughes of Connah's Quay took me to her. We had to take our own bedding. We did the coastal trade, mostly carrying iron, scrap or stone. It was a fair paying job of about £1 per month wage – that's a month, not a week, mind. We worked four hours on and four off. There was plenty of room for our crew of four hands and it was as rough or as pleasurable as you made it. But trading with the French ports was fun.

In bad winds with the sea breaking above your head, you held onto that wheel for the sake of your life and your crew's lives as well. You would be soaked to the skin, with clothes that weighed five times their usual weight. I was just thirteen years old when I first went to sea, and coming off watch in soaking wet clothes I'd drop on the bed and sleep until someone shook we awake and it was time to cook or to get to the wheel again.

We were hit off Dover and I can remember it as if it were yesterday. We were wind bound with another Connah's Quay ship, the *Windermere*, and a tramp steamer came at us dragging her anchor. She missed the *Windermere*, but took our bowsprit and part of the bulwark off, and we had to signal for a tow to port. On the night it happened there was so bright a moon that you could have picked a pin off the deck. The steamer was called the *Ibex*, I recall her name now. We were very lucky that there were no injuries on our ship that night. It took six weeks to repair that ship and then I came home to Connah's Quay.

A real bad winter was murder on a schooner. On still, cold nights, you could see the ropes and lines tightening as the frost took a hold. The crew might be up all night trying to keep the ship free of ice. We had a bit of a fire up in the fo'castle, but not enough to dry you out after a soaking. Remember, there was no cover over the wheel like on some later ships – these schooners were stripped to the basics for speed. You might have to force a brush handle through the wheel so as to hold her on a rough sea, and you often looked up to see a wave way above your head, sometimes higher than a modern two-storey house.'

Food was on the whole very good, mostly burgo biscuits with weevils living in them. You knocked the biscuit and they fell out, then you ate the biscuit. We had fresh meat from local butchers brought to the dockside, and the trick was to salt it properly. What you did was to fill a barrel with water then add salt and a piece of potato. If the spud floated then you had enough salt, if it sank you had too much. We mainly used brisket-beef – it was the cheapest and best.

I can't recall many grumbles about the food from the crew. They had enough to grumble about with the weather, without starting on the cook. The *Margaret Hobley* was about one hundred and fifty tons. My next ship was the *Anne of Barrow*, again from Connah's Quay and she was about the same weight.

During the First World War I was an able-bodied seaman from out of Point of Air on the *Fowey*. We took coal from the Point to France and the ship was a sixty-four share ship that anyone could buy. We mostly carried coal and then sometimes a general sort of cargo on the return trip for the east coast of England, or to one of the channel ports.

After leaving her I went to the *Lady Moyra*, a paddle steamer that was used to sweep mines. We went into Torquay one time and she was the biggest ship that they ever had had in there. There was just six-feet remaining on either side when she berthed – it was very, very tight.

We swept the channel by day and the Germans re-laid them at night. It was a terrible experience on the minesweepers because you saw other ships being blown-up all around you, and wondered when it was to be your turn. These paddle steamers had a shallow draught that they said would travel over the mines because they were set low in the water, but reality was something else.

One night a Zeppelin was brought down near the Tongue Light Vessel and two trawlers got a line to her to save her sinking. We were to take her in-tow for the 'top-brass' to examine at Margate Sands. But we developed engine and boiler trouble and the crew was paid-off. I then went to join the *Desiree*.

Sometimes we went out as far as five hundred miles to pick-up a convoy. One dark rough night off Kinsale, Southern Ireland, we were in a convoy when the leading ship took a mine and exploded. It shook our ship so badly we thought that we had been hit as well. I had a boat lowered but it was so dark that we could only trace the survivors by calling down to them and they calling back. We saved seven from its crew of thirty-one. I saw something white and massive in amongst the bits of wreckage and it was a huge cod, the biggest I'd ever seen. It was deeply appreciated, as our rations were very low. We took the survivors to just off Holyhead, where they were transferred to another ship for Liverpool.

I was promoted to Second Hand whilst sweeping the channel and whilst we were there, we saw my old ship the *Fowey*. They signalled to tell her I was there, which was nice of them, especially at such a hectic time.

Whilst I was on the *James Evans* we had to light flares in an effort to keep the German subs out of the area. It was a very dangerous job and we were all terrified. A hand came aboard who seemed a very odd man and nobody knew anything about him. I tried to get to know him but failed. Then one night he asked me if I knew a Welsh village called Sychdyn. I said that I did and we became good mates.

*James Evans* was a big trawler out of the Quay. We were washing her decks in dock one day when the crew yelled that they were getting wet. The caulkers had forgotten to do the deck and the water ran between the wooden boarding, drenching everyone below. Once that was put right, we were off to the channel again.

After the war finished, I came home fully paid-up and looking for work. I went to Runcorn and the *Black Cat* and it was heaven to be back amongst the sails, and away from those dirty smelly steamers. We carried a lot of clay and bricks from all over the place. She was sold in 1920 which was when I left her. She was a bit under-rated to carry coal and I later heard that she had in fact gone down whilst carrying coal. It was very sad indeed.

I had £2 a month on the *Black Cat* and my job was mending the sail. That was a job. It made your hands hard and sore with needle pricks, not to mention making you ill tempered.

Connah's Quay docks had four hand-cranes as well as steam-cranes, but they were old and slow. The loading rates were ½d per ton to load or unload, and out of port it was 1½ pence. I had a chit for my ship the *Isabella* but I've lost it, and that was 4/-d loading fee.

There were large coal-sidings there and carthorses pulled the trucks off the main line in the sidings. Beautiful animals they were, all shiny brasses. They went into shows sometimes. Of course there was a massive brick and pipe trade from there all over the world, and I remember seeing ships four or five deep alongside. There was a bad problem with the channel changing. They had a dredger there, but it got so bad at times that the channel was re-perched almost every tide.

I remember one ship I was in owned by Hancocks of Buckley, the famous pipemakers. I complained that she was overloaded and the overseer came and looked and called to the man with the horses: 'Fetch two trucks but one will do.' Tonnage meant money and trying to convince the loaders that there were safety limits was impossible. Cargo and cash came first and safety rules were a poor second.

I've seen the river at the Quay blocked with so many ships so that none could get past to Chester or down to the sea. Nobody would move as there was always another ship standing-off somewhere, waiting for a berth. Space was money and there was always a race against time.

If you look downstream to where Connah's Quay power station is today, that area at low water was full of ships high and dry, being repaired. There were men on ladders, caulking between the wooden planks with pitch, or scraping or painting. Apart from the repairs, there were also some very fine ships built at Connah's Quay.

Saltney, the Quay and Mostyn were all busy ports in their day. Connah's Quay had an excellent reputation for a fast turn-round and it was much sought after by owners of cargoes. But weather governed everything out of the Chester river. We left Connah's Quay laden with bricks one day for Ireland. We were with two other schooners, the *Charles & Ellen* and the *Moss Rose*, and it was a bit blowy. When we reached Wild Roads (off Talacre) we hit really bad weather and we tried to run for the Skerries, but it was too bad. Off Moelfre we met *Ford Fisher*, *Pearl* and *Isabella* all trying to get to Ireland laden, but it was hopeless.

On the Sunday it was so bad that we called for a lifeboat to take us ashore and we left the ships out at anchor. *Pearl* got free and the wind got in her sails and grounded her at Red Wharf Bay. She was pulled away by tugs undamaged later on. It was the following Friday before we got back to the ships and then we had to pump them out. It was a terrible time we had and cost the owners a packet in lost trade.

People can't imagine now what it was like on those old schooners in bad weather. I remember as a lad somewhere off Dover trying to take in a sail, and I was on the bowsprit. The waves were crashing over me, even up there, but any loose canvas meant that the wind might take her where you didn't want her to go. I've seen many a ship limping back into the Quay with a broken bowsprit or damaged bulwark, done mostly in this estuary. It is no place to fool about.

It was in 1932 that I became a ship-owner. I bought the *Isabella* off W H Stephenson from Plymouth and I traded her around the coast carrying all sorts of cargoes. We had a good time together and when I sold her the new owners fitted an engine, but she was not built for that and it proved it. They sold her as a yacht.

I was also a Pilot on the Chester river. We charged 2/7d per foot length and picked up the ships off Great Orme's Head, off Llandudno. The pilot ship was motorised and we took three or four in-tow at a time at over one hundred and fifty tons a piece. Some stood-off at Mostyn and discharged onto *flats* which were taken into the various ports by smaller boats. We had eleven pilots on the river then, and we pooled the monies until the end of the month. It was very busy then.

There was a big tugboat on the river, the *Manxman*, owned I think by the railway company, which caused all manner of problems. She had a huge searchlight fitted that was forever handy. I think she came up here from Milford Haven. There were problems with some tugs it was true, but getting the ship-owners to pay their dues was another matter.,'

Some of the smaller ports were bad to get in and out of. Bagillt was bad, with just one long jetty and the water went so shallow at the mouth that you could ground there even on a good tide. It was also difficult to tie-up there because of the way it was built. To be honest I tried to avoid that one and Dee Banks gutter, which was no better. If some difficult chap came behind you, it was not easy to persuade him to allow you to get away on a tide. Fflint was another bad port – another long one with no turning room for bigger ships and bad unloading facilities. People tried to stay away from these. Mostyn and Quay were all right, and Summers Wharf and Saltney, except it was busy. Chester had a few ports there and they were all right, provided the tide was running good and high. In hot weather they ran quieter and low, if there was no wind to ship them up. It could be murder even on a tide of 27 feet, and there was not time to waste getting under-way at all.

We didn't do much with livestock up here, but when we carried from St Catherine's dock in London to Belgium, they'd kill a load of horses in London and we carried the meat across, fresh for eating. It was a well-paid trade and needed a fast boat for the job. But it didn't please me – not horses.

Hides and skins were a good paying trade but the smell on the raw or green hides was unmentionable. I did try to miss them if I could, but a load was a load and that was money. But after they were unloaded the hold stank for ages, no matter how well it was cleaned-off.

Summers had the last fleet on this river, although there were some ships working out of here until the mid-1960s. But once the line from the brickworks was closed, then the trade died off. Summers needed bigger boats to get steel away and raw materials in, so they used the road from Birkenhead docks.

I worked on the *Stalybridge* for Summers and when they said she was being sold, I left and went inside on the steam-shunters. That's where I finished work. It was painful to watch those schooners tied alongside the quay here, just going up and down on the tide. Then some were taken to be broken-up and others rotted away. The river was dead and nobody seemed to want to know. But in fairness Summers did look after the dockers and crews, taking most of them in and giving them a job. I think it was 1966 that the last ship worked out of here.

I remember the herring in the estuary. They came in good numbers each year then suddenly they stopped coming. They said it was over-fishing, but I honestly think it was just their nature to move suddenly away for no known reason. Many of the older ones talked of herring rotting on the quayside as they were so abundant, then they were scarce, and then abundant again. You didn't know who or what to believe. But certainly salted herring was on the menu of most ships and there were ships hereabout that worked for nothing else. Most of the time herring was there just for the asking.

It's the same with salmon and sea trout – nothing like the numbers come-up now as once did. Connah's Quay dock was thick with people watching them run upstream as the tide fell-back. Now, not even the nets take many, but I've seen fifty or more taken in one net at a time. But the salmon are being poached and netted out on the high seas and that's why we can't catch them here anymore. You can't catch what won't run up river can you.

I see people being charged a fortune for keeping a small boat in the dock now and it isn't right at all. Nobody should be charged. I can still see those big beautiful carthorses on the dockside pulling coaches, and I still see the sails being taken down and stored alongside, and the crews running to get away home. I remember two wooden ships being broken-up and one of them sank a sub in the last war, but that seemed to count for nothing – a little old sail-ship against a mighty iron submarine.

I think of those old smelly steamers and the sweet silent sailing-ships that were low and fast, and the biscuit and weevils. Herring was a treat out at sea and if you were very lucky you had bacon on a Sunday morning for breakfast, proper bacon with a good inch or more back fat on it – not the rubbish we buy now.

If I could turn the clock back I'd go to sea again tomorrow, provided they gave me a sailing ship and not a greasy, smelly steamer.

# Bob Edwards – Master Mariner

Bob Edwards is a retired master mariner who was friendly with Joe Fellows and Bob Manifold but, unlike them, never took to the sail-ships. He was a steam and diesel man. In his opinion the days of sail are best gone because the old schooners were a nightmare, relying as they did on the whims of the wind. They were helpless in a gale whereas a diesel-powered ship can cut into or across a wind, even when laden. Sentiment over the sail-ships was useless because his ships could make six trips a week to Ireland, irrespective of the weather. A schooner might make one in ten days, and less if it was becalmed. After twenty-seven years as a Captain on the Dee, he also had his memories.

* * *

I remember as a lad that there was a gutter running into the Dee from by Rockcliffe Hall that was used by ships or flats to take grain to Kelsterton Brewery. Casks of ale were sent out on the returning flats to bigger ships at anchor in the Dee. Ships also took passengers up to Chester or wherever, rather than use the road or railway system.

My grandfather ran flats that each carried sixty or seventy tons of stone. The stone came from a quarry in Rock Road, between Connah's Quay and Fflint and they used stone from the same quarry to make the causeway there. They also used the flats to carry stone to make and support the banking at Saltney in the Higher Ferry area. It was amazing how many people came down and asked if they could send their produce up to Chester on the flats, as it was such a quick route.

As a lad I'd play about on the dock at Connah's Quay and watch the old sail ships coming and going, and see them drop ballast in the shallows. After the tide had gone out we'd play on the stones that had been dropped from the ships.

My grandfather's name was John Latham. He had fishing boats and would fish all over the estuary. People go on about the decline in fish stocks in the estuary today, and this is largely true. In my grandfather's day they made good catches, but there was not the same amount of poaching on the river as there is today. Every Tom, Dick and Harry is out there netting whatever swims, with no regard for the seasons or anything. You see them out there on any state of the tide, by day and by night, netting away and nothing stands a chance.

I remember the *Water Witch* and the *Janet* taking tar from the stage at Queensferry up to the old gasworks at Chester. This was a regular trip and people went for a ride or a business trip into Chester. Plenty of locally grown produce went on those ships to Chester market and brought good prosperity to the small farmers and market gardeners. The old bones of the *Water Witch* and *Janet* are up by Bob Manifold's house somewhere, where they were broken-up. They were of a type they called the 'Northwich Barge', being of shallow draught.

I don't remember much going on at Saltney Wharf, though everyone talked about how busy it was in days gone by. I do remember the horses there, pulling coal-wagons that were tipped directly into the ships. They had horses at Connah's Quay and at Point of Air as well. I can clearly remember seeing that big grain elevator built up at the Ferry, and I saw it being towed away and out to sea. There was also a good trade in explosives between Queensferry and the West Indies and the East Indies as well as I recall. There was always something of a panic when one of the explosive ships came into the port to be loaded. Red flags flew and everyone stayed well clear.

I was sixteen when I went fishing with the family fleet, and then I went to work on the John Summers & Sons boats from the ironwork's wharf. You know about the *Barron Hill* that lies off Fflint? On the night she sank I was with my grandfather and there was such a fierce gale that we were forced to leave a flat in the gutter at Pentre (the old Roman dock area) until the next tide.

The *Barron Hill* was a three-mast ship and she was tight on the sandbanks and refused to move, but because of the gale it was too dangerous to try for long. On the next tide she came a bit, then broke her back and that was the end. Grounding out there is so easy – I know because I did it myself. I was an AB on the *Felita* when she grounded in rough weather. I'd just missed the channel because it changed so frequently that it was almost impossible to chart the damn thing. It was a bitch of a night with stormy winds and rain. The cargo shifted and she went over to almost 45degrees, and we thought we'd had it. I went out with the engineers and we tried to reset the tarpaulins – it was terrifying. God only knows why or how, but she stayed as she was and on the next tide just righted herself and we were quickly away. It was a very long night. But if we hadn't tried to reset that cargo she'd have broken her back and gone down, maybe taking us with her.

The next fright I had from grounding was when the pilot completely missed the channel, and she stuck fast aft. She was swinging about in the bad winds and we feared for the worst, but we got her away on the next tide. Her bottom was so damaged it had to be renewed though.

I was the Master on Summers' *Stalybridge* for seventeen and a half years, and I can honestly say I that loved every minute of it. We carried a lot of pig iron from Shotton to Cardiff, and also up to Workington and Barrow. It was when we went around Hilbre that we saw the seals on the sandbanks and if we had to drop anchor there overnight, then they would come alongside the ship as if they were attracted by the lights. If you rattled a teapot whilst emptying it, they'd come to see what was going on. They were very odd indeed. I have seen as many as one hundred and sixty with young on the Hoyle-bank there.

I was once out on a flat with a member of the Catherine family. The father and brother were on the ketch *Squirrel* in the basin opposite The Olde Quay House pub at Connah's Quay, and she grounded as she turned. She was real fast and a danger to other shipping. A steam-train working in the docks was somehow connected to her and the train was to pull her clear, but her old wood broke and the captain fell into the water. His son dived in to help him and I clearly heard the captain shout 'You'll have to be quick', but when the son got there his father had gone. It was some months before his body was found in the stanchions of the Wrexham – Bidston railway bridge across the Dee.

I was here all through the war. There was a Navy patrol out of Mostyn checking everything that moved up or down stream, and they dictated what flag we flew. I'll tell you something else that was keen – the pilots from the airfields near here. They used ships on the river for dummy-run target-practise, and when you saw those planes coming at you from the clouds, you sometimes wondered whether they were theirs or ours. They used all sizes of crafty from the small fishing-boats to the big sea-going vessels. There were some German planes shot-down on the estuary and I remember one coming down just over the training-wall and sinking in a few minutes. Some prisoners were taken but a few drowned in the mud and silt. It wasn't pleasant being out on an evening tide either, because that was when the Germans came for Liverpool from the Irish Sea. After a bombing run they'd drop any bombs that were left on anything that moved in the sea. They could obviously fly faster and use less fuel without a payload.

The fog was probably the most frightening thing on the estuary. It didn't roll-in, as they say; it fell like a stone and if you were looking for a channel-marker or a buoy or something, it was often too late and you were stuck. Grounding in itself wasn't too bad but you need to realise that in those days the estuary was very busy and whereas you seemed tight and safe, there was always the possibility of being rammed by someone who couldn't see you.

By the end of Connah's Quay docks, I was acting as a Pilot out of

Mostyn. It was Liverpool that took away the trade in the 1960s, because of the silting and the lack of modern equipment at our ports. Also the size of our ships couldn't compare to the Mersey. I was actually on the last ship out of Fflint dock – the *Felita*. That was a pig of a port to get in and out of, just a straight jetty and it was so easy to get blocked in. If a big ship came in, they had to back-out and hope for the best with the channel and the nasty sandbanks at the mouth of the dock. Fflint and Bagillt and some of the others were hell, but Connah's Quay was easy.

It was the selling-off of the pipe and brick-works that killed Connah's Quay. They hung on to the last, but by then there were pleasure yachts as big as some ships that worked out of the Quay.

I think that a museum about shipping on the Dee would be a great idea and I hope I'm here long enough to see it. The Dee estuary hasn't always been the muddy place it is today and its maritime history is very important. It's a story that needs telling. Few estuaries in the United Kingdom can have the history of this one, or have seen the tonnage of goods moved that this one saw. And then there's the wildlife that has come here. But everyone wants to use the Dee as a dustbin. It's crazy, it really is.

# Airfields

### Broughton
Before it became an airfield in 1939, the site at Hawarden was a massive agricultural field of reclaimed land. The airfield was built for the construction of Wellington bombers, and was soon working in tandem with the nearby Poulton aerodrome on the Westminster Estate, near the Cheshire banks of the Dee.

It is easy to see why the government accepted Hawarden as a site. It fitted the criteria of being near large built-up areas, making it accessible because of nearby rail, road and river facilities. But because Hawarden was vulnerable to German bombing because of its proximity to Liverpool, a large dummy airfield was built just outside Saltney called 'Decoy Farm', complete with hangers and old vehicles to make it look as if the place was a properly run airfield. It wasn't and it didn't attract German bombers.

The Government had decreed in 1935 that, in the event of war, there must be shadow factories throughout the country near large population areas. These were to be capable of quickly turning out parts, engines and operational aircraft. Broughton was chosen in1937, and work soon began on the site. The contractor was W Arrol & Sons of Clydeside; the same people as built Queensferry Bridge in 1926. Most of the adjoining land belonging to Hawarden Estates (Gladstone family) was acquired by compulsory purchase, an entire farm was demolished and many ponds were filled-in to accommodate a landing strip.

In the middle of 1938 over one-third of the population of Mold was out of work and the new airfield was a welcome arrival. Hawarden Rural District Council built Broughton village with suitable housing, and the workforce was expanded. In 1939 the airfield was again enlarged, taking in a second farm that was also pulled down, and more ponds were filled in. It was soon realised that all the pond filling was denying the site of natural drainage, because the entire site resembled a swamp.

The first order came in 1939, for 750 Wellington bombers, followed by a further order for 1,583 bombers. Flooding was so bad however that assembled Wellingtons had to be flown to Weybridge for proper testing. Having built the 'dummy'airfield south of Saltney, it was assumed that any daytime German bombers would fly in from the south, and hopefully see the 'dummy' before seeing Broughton. The dummy airfield was made to look like a night-flying base, complete with a lit runway and even had a cinder-path car park with old vehicles on it. Examination from the air said that Broughton's camouflage was complete. Another 'decoy' was set-up at Buckley, this one made to look like a badly blacked-out factory, which was set up by hanging lanterns behind perforated screens. Neither of the 'dummy' sites were bombed, and it became apparent after the war that Broughton was not listed on German maps, but Summers steelworks was as was Sealand airfield. Recent research however suggests that the Germans did know about Broughton, but could not find it. There was one attack on Broughton on September 14, 1940, but the other bombs that fell were dropped by accident following raids on Liverpool, when the German bombers wanted a fast get away from the pursuing British fighters. There were frequent incidents as they fought over the Dee and Sealand as well as inland Flintshire and Denbighshire.

Air Transport Auxiliary opened at Broughton in May 1940. Its object was to use amateur pilots, or those who couldn't fly on active service for medical reasons, to fly aircraft from Broughton to other parts of the country, thus freeing more pilots for active duties. It started with just twenty-six pilots but had over six hundred at its peak, ninety of these being female. They flew everything from light trainers to bombers, and lost one hundred and fifty-six staff during the whole of the war.

By June 1940 there was also an operational training unit at Broughton commanded by Wing Commander J R Hallings-Pott DSO. Their first fatality was a Hurricane, which stalled and crashed over Holywell. Some pilots had as little as ten hours training on Spitfires or Hurricanes before they went into battle.

At this time the north-west had no fighter cover, with the main force being concentrated on East Anglia and the Home Counties. Hallings-Potts decided that this had to change and three fully armed Spitfires were stationed at Broughton, just in case. They drew first blood on August 14, 1940 when a German bomber was shot down just after it bombed Sealand airfield. Squadron Leader J S McLean was drinking in a tent with Hallings-Potts when they heard the bombs explode at Sealand. They forced the Heinkel to make a landing at Border Farm, Saltney and the German crew surrendered to the local home-guard (Bob Manifold was one of the Home Guard who arrested the crew after they had set fire to their aeroplane). A second Heinkel was discovered whilst chasing the first over Sealand, and this crash-landed near Machynlleth after receiving heavy fire over Meirionnydd. The crew of four was captured. The same Spitfire crew later shot down a DO 17 over Anglesey, after it had dropped bombs on Liverpool.

Hawarden Castle was requisitioned as an Officers Mess and Manor Farm as a transport section, and work began on improving the runway and the rest of the airfield. But in the autumn of 1940, the tents were flooded again and the Flintshire Police Force visited every house in the area seeking accommodation for the airmen. Many spent the nights on the floors of houses, for which the home-owner received six-pence a night.

On the night of November 14, 1940, Coventry was severely bombed, many German bombers then breaking formation to look for other targets. Bombs fell on a hanger at Broughton damaging twenty-eight aircraft, this being the only known deliberate raid of the war. The only other attack was in February 1941 when an anti-aircraft shell (of British make) fell on a hanger and exploded, damaging two aircraft.

By December 1940, the airfield was unusable due to flooding because all the drainage had been filled-in and the water had nowhere to run. The result was that a huge ditch was dug to drain the land, and this helped. Following the lift in bad weather, two new runways were built crossways.

There was also some fun at Broughton. They had an ex-cavalry officer there who insisted on charging about on a huge white horse, apparently terrifying the airmen. There was some relief when the ageing animal died, until a party was detailed to bury the damn thing.

Another funny story is that of the trainees who had to stabilise aircraft on the field by lying across the tail and then dropping off just as they taxied for take-off. One chap it seems was a mite slow in getting off and the aircraft took off with him on board. The pilot, realising something was wrong, circled high over Chester with the poor lad straddling the tail section (which was a rather flimsy affair). The pilot saw what was wrong and landed safely. It was said that the poor chap on the back was so afraid that they had to force his fingers so as to release his grip on the plane. Thankfully, he recovered.

Another tale is about a flight engineer who was to fly with a pilot of whom he was unsure. The engineer was putting on a greatcoat when the pilot remarked, 'There's no need for a greatcoat on a sunny day like this.'

, 'No,' the engineer replied, 'but it could be cold in the back of an ambulance coming back.' All well in love and war.

There are countless stories of aircraft returning on a wing and a prayer, and of crash landings in appalling weather. Pilots were lost on training and accidents, but by July 1945 Broughton became storage for Wellingtons and Halifaxes that, although they continued to make them, were taken onto the airfield and then scrapped. At one time there were over one thousand bombers in storage at Broughton and Hooton, awaiting the axe. It must have been a distressing time for the crews and the work force which, at its height in the war, numbered over seven thousand (a lot of them being ladies). When production came to an end in 1945, five thousand five hundred and forty Wellingtons had been assembled at Broughton, and a further six hundred were cancelled at the end of hostilities.

Following the war, pre-fab houses had been made using steel from near-by Summers but, in 1948, De Havilands came to Broughton and aircraft production started again. De Havilands had twelve test pilots on their books by 1953, testing Vampires, Venoms, Doves and Herons and the place was full of aircraft awaiting test flight. In 1958 the RAF closed their operations there and moved to Sealand, and De Havilands took over their hangers as well.

By 1962 the highly impressive civilian aircraft the DH 125 was in full production. The following year, De Havilands became Hawker-Siddeley and it was the success of the 125 that kept the factory going.

'Starways' of Liverpool started a passenger service to London in 1963, but trips to the Isle of Man were dropped. By 1965 however the total number of passengers had risen to over eighteen thousand. The runway was supposed to have been lengthened in 1966 but the cancellation of the passenger service put an end to that. By December 1969 the service had been revived but the company lost a lot of money and the route was closed in April 1970.

Today, the factory is part of the British Aerospace company. There have been mass redundancies but they now make the wings for the A300 airbus. There is also work done on smaller aircraft. Much of the old wartime complex off Manor Lane is now an industrial site and some of the old wartime hangers are used for private storage. The sister site at Pulton has largely been returned to agricultural use, as it was in the pre 1939 era. The concrete is broken by the heat and cold, and weeds push through the rusting buildings and cracking runways as nature goes through the process of reclaiming what was rightfully hers in the first place.

**Royal Air Force Base, Sealand**
The two hundred and fifty acres of land controlled by the RAF at Sealand was reclaimed from the sea following the canalization in the 18th century. It was used only for agriculture until a private individual sought to obtain permission to start a flying school in 1915, with one aircraft. There was some disagreement but it was sanctioned, and in 1917 when the Ministry was looking for suitable land as an air base, the area was placed under the control of the Royal Flying Corp.

In the First World War there was a need to train pilots as quickly as possible for active service, mostly in France, and it was to Sealand that many came to learn how to control their aircraft. Following the minimum of training they were sent to France, often ill equipped and with an average life expectancy of just a few hours.

Although some called the original site Shotwick, it was mostly known as Queensferry. It was from here that, in a long wooden shed holding just four aircraft, the serious business of training began. The area that had been rented to a Mr T Murray Dutton was not big enough for the needs of the Flying Corp as more and more aircraft had to be moved north to escape any attacks on the south and south-east of England. A site was also needed near the port of Liverpool for shipping parts and aircraft, and Queensferry was the obvious choice.

Much of the initial work done on the site was by German prisoners of war and Irish labourers. Robert McAlpine of Queensferry was given the contract to build living accommodation for eight hundred and thirty nine people, including two hundred and nine women, at a cost of £350,000. Six aeroplane storage sheds and a repair shed were also built. The site then covered 165 acres of land with a landing area of 1,000 yards, but as it was only 15 feet above sea level it raised problems with drainage and flooding.

On October 22 1917, No 37 Wing was formed at Ledsham on the Wirral and then moved to Queensferry. Within twelve months 90 Squadron had also moved there from Shawbury. By April 1918 they had three classes of trainer there. Class 'A' – 6 Avros. Class 'B' – 6 Sopwith Pups. Class 'C' – 2 Dolphins.

Following of World War I there was a rail strike in 1919 causing problems in distributing the mail. Most of the mail for the north of England was flown to Queensferry and then distributed from there, or flown on to other parts of the country. Many ex-World War I pilots were engaged in flying the mail. Parachutes were not distributed until 1926, and a pilot had no chance whatsoever if a minor fault occurred, let alone an enemy shooting bits off the flimsy machines.

Sealand was reshaped again in 1927 with a further eighty flying pupils taken on. The old sheds were torn down and replaced, and four types of trainer were introduced instead of the outdated Auro 504N trainer. These were the Auro Gosport, Auro Avian, De Haviland Gipsy Moth and the Hawker Tomtit. The Gipsy Moth and the Tomtit were big favourites.

In 1929 the RAF packing-department arrived on site from Ascot to pack and crate aircraft for overseas, mainly from Birkenhead, Liverpool or Ellesmere Port.

In February 1931, twenty-six officers and eleven airmen passed-out having gained their wings, including a Sergeant Scragg who went on to become an Air Vice-Marshal. On June 24 of that year, two Americans named Wiley Post and Harold Gatty attempting to fly around the world in ten days, landed at Sealand for an engine check and a refuel. They went on to complete the task a day short of the ten.

On May 24 1934 the first ever 'Empire Day' was held at Sealand with the public being admitted and the grand sum of £151.5.9d was raised for the RAF Benevolent Funds. It was in the same year that expansion targets for the RAF began to be met. But bad weather and high winds, and the increasing congestion in the skies made Sealand a poor site to increase its training capabilities. The numbers of trainees sent there were accordingly reduced to coincide with other airfields being opened elsewhere.

On November 24, 1936 Colonel Charles Lindbergh, probably the most famous round the world flyer, was forced down at Sealand by fog. It was four days before conditions improved, during which time he prepared the aircraft for departure. By way of the deep appreciation he felt for his treatment, he presented the staff with a solid silver rose-bowl that is still displayed in the camp today.

The clouds of war darkened again over Europe during the 1930s, and the number of aircraft built in Britain dramatically increased. Ships carried as many as fifteen planes at a time from Sealand, where they were packed in crates. Their crews were sent by ship from the Merseyside ports, mostly to the Middle East. The land adjacent to the A550 was acquired in 1937 and Sealand was quickly expanded.

No 30 Maintenance Unit was brought to Sealand in 1939, under the direction of Squadron-Leader Chamberlain. Military equipment that was repaired included wireless gear and aircraft spares. They were then sent overseas. One of the first ships sunk in World War II was the SS *Manaar*, which was carrying crated 'Swordfish' and 'Wellesley' planes. It was suspected at the time that the Germans had received information as to her cargo and from whence it came, but nothing has ever been officially proven. The winter of 1939/40 was very severe, causing flood problems due to the low-lying position of the base.

Soon after midnight on June 28, 1940 a German aircraft was heard overhead and the entire station was put on alert. Two bombs fell near the officers' mess, damaging the nearby buildings and shattering windows, but with no loss of life. In an effort to combat further air-attacks, fighter cover was stationed at Sealand (as it was at Hawarden). The number of Hurricanes 11A's packed at the base was increased. They were sent mostly by sea to the Dutch East Indies. In the end, even the cover aircraft were stripped and packed for transportation.

On August 14, 1940 German bombers attacked the base for the second time. Three Heinkel 111's were dispatched from Luftflotte 3, based in Western France, to attack outlying airfields. The first plane dropped eight high-explosive bombs and one incendiary bomb in a straight line on Sealand. Following the initial bombing run the bomber then machine-gunned the base. Technically it was bad bombing, but it did some damage. The bombers were unescorted, which gives some degree of their confidence of air superiority.

Having completed its mayhem the first bomber gave way for the second plane to drop a total of nine bombs causing damage to the site, electricity cables and a recently completed roadway. A Warrant Officer was killed as was a horse grazing in a nearby field. Hurricanes were dispatched from Hawarden. They couldn't stop the planes causing considerable damage but two of the Heinkels were shot down and the crews captured.

During September 1940 there were one hundred and sixty-two alerts at Sealand as German bombers sought out Liverpool. This curtailed the night-flying activities considerably, including training. Sealand suffered no more bomb attacks however, but one thousand four hundred and fifty-three people were killed in Liverpool.

America was not yet in the War, but Americans were enlisting as airmen and many came to Sealand. British Government news-reel recordings were made and radio interviews were carried out, with the Americans sending personal messages back home to loved ones, and attempts were made to get their fellow countrymen to follow and enlist.

By 1941 the Sealand base was so effective at packing aircraft that a plane flown in mid-morning could be broken and packed away by mid-afternoon. Birkenhead soon became a discharge port as Liverpool docks were badly damaged by bombing. They were also risky because the Germans were bombing day and night. Another system was to send crated planes out on flats to where ships lay-off at anchor. The crates were then winched on board. This was a familiar sight off the Dee and Mersey estuaries during World War II.

One hundred and four aircraft were packed in November 1942 and 145 in December. By then, they were also making their own packing crates. The operation reached a peak in April 1943 when a total of two hundred and forty four aircraft, including Spitfires, Hurricanes, Beauforts, Magisters, Proctor 111's, Austers, Mosquito's and Typhoons were shipped out.

Sealand continued to train pilots throughout the war but it was maintenance and the packing of aircraft that mainly employed the staff. The grass runway did not last well because of the volume of incoming aircraft to be packed and a 3,960 foot runway was constructed in 1941 because of the wear on the grass. Lancaster bombers were then flown in for repair, and the staff was strengthened by the arrival of Polish crews. But work on the Lancaster was slow due to the lack of knowledge and a lack of spare parts.

In October 1945 the base returned to training. In 1946 the total strength dropped from four thousand to one thousand and a relative tranquillity returned to Sealand.

The Americans had meanwhile built Burtonwood to be one of the largest military bases in Britain. But as pressures increased on Burtonwood during the Berlin airlift of 1949, Sealand became important again. The United States Air Force used Sealand as a main storage base for the British operations because of the proximity of Liverpool and Birkenhead docks. The important fringe benefits for the area were American dollars. There was only limited flying activity at Sealand, and the base came under review by the USAF in 1956 and closed on July 1, 1957.

This came as a terrible blow to the locally recruited civilian staff and to the general Deeside economy. Mrs Eirene White MP raised the matter in the House of Commons and the Ministry agreed to take another look at the base's possibilities.

As a result it was reopened in October 1958 as No. 41 Group Maintenance Command. By June 1959 there was a compliment of nine hundred and twelve staff comprising of twenty-four Officers, fifty-six non-commissioned officers, three hundred and twenty-four airmen, fifteen civilians with officer status and four hundred and ninety-three other civilians.

RAF Sealand employed twelve hundred civilians and six hundred and fifty servicemen in 1978, on a site of just over 2,500 acres. They were responsible for the maintenance of military equipment and radios. Today Sealand is still concerned with the repair of radio and other ancillary equipment for the RAF. There is still a runway on West Camp but it is rarely used other than by the odd helicopter. The RAF VR also maintain No. 631 Gliding School there at weekends. Part of the base has been demolished to enlarge the Deeside Industrial Estate and it seems that in time this could be the fate of the base-one large operational Industrial Estate.

# The Lifeboats and Lighthouses on the river Dee

Grenville Collins first properly charted the Dee estuary in 1690. Before this, the estuary had been a ship's graveyard as the Dee cut its twisted course from the estuary up to Chester docks. The shifting sandbanks with every tide and few ships ventured out at night because of this.

A meeting was held at Chester on November 24th 1775 to discuss the problem, and the assembled company demanded an Act of Parliament to cover the erection of a light tower near Point of Air. The London Company of Cheese-makers gave evidence that their losses on the Dee were more than £40,000. But the port of Liverpool, then in its infancy, objected that a light might attract shipping away from the Mersey.

The Act was passed in 1776 and a wooden lighthouse was built at Point of Air. It had two tar buckets on a flat platform at the top of a 35 foot tower. A man was employed to act as keeper and Sir Peter Mostyn, the landowner, received 2shillings per annum for his trouble. He even retained the right to hire and fire as he pleased. Public subscriptions flowed in once it was revealed that more two hundred lives had recently been lost in the estuary. This was in addition to a vast amount of valuable cargo.

By September 30, 1777 the light-tower was up and running at a cost of

£353.18.4d. The first keeper on the north-Wales coast was Edward Price who received three weeks training at one of the Liverpool towers. His job at Point of Air was to maintain the tar buckets so that one light showing to the Orme's head, and a second to Heswall.

Sadly, it was not successful. The flames were more visible in daylight than at night because of the wind. The pitch froze solid in cold weather and the thick smoke hid the flames in rough weather, making the tower more visible from the inland side than the seaward side. This caused problem with the collection of dues from ship owners, who justifiably complained that ships were still grounding on the sandbanks and that the light should be more efficient.

A light-ship was moored out on the estuary but this was not that much better. The ever-shifting sands of the Dee moved at Point of Air until, in 1860, the light-tower eventually fell into the sea. A larger and stronger metal replaced it in 1863. In 1903 a better light-ship was moored at the point where the Dee buoy is moored today. This was fitted with a gong and a white light that showed every ten seconds.

The current lighthouse is a tourist attraction. It saw a limited amount of service before it was withdrawn in the 1920s. The lighthouse was, they claimed, too far inland to be of any use and by the time it was seen the ships were almost aground. £20,000 was spent on converting it into a second home in the 1960s, but it was never completed. There was a building attached to the base of this lighthouse as lately as 1958, of which there is no trace today. Nothing is known of the old metal tower, but it is assumed that it fell into the sea at some point.

The Royal National Institution for the Preservation of Life from Shipwreck was founded in 1824. Hoylake had a lightweight lifeboat since 1803 but had to put to sea into the prevalent westerly winds. There was therefore plenty of evidence to support a claim for a lifeboat at Point of Air. This arrived in 1824 in the shape of a 40 feet long boat with a crew of thirteen, and life jackets donated by Liverpool Docks Committee. Manning the boat was a problem because of the sparse population. Robert Beck and John Sherlack, both being professional seamen, came from Hoylake to assist. They were given an allowance in return for their loss of fishing. The rest of the crew was made up of carpenters, colliers, labourers and gardeners, a shopkeeper and a sawyer.

On the morning of January 7, 1857 disaster struck. A distress call was received to the effect that two small crafts had grounded off Abergele and that a Sloop was sinking off Prestatyn. A further report was received about a Brig, *The Temperance of Belfast*, being in serious trouble off Pensarn.

Both the Point of Air and Rhyl lifeboat were launched. The men of Point left their cork jackets because they were too heavy and did nothing to aid a swimming man. The people of Rhyl, standing on the dunes, witnessed a huge wave throwing the Point of Air lifeboat onto her back, catapulting the crew of thirteen into the freezing sea. Three men could be seen clinging to the side of the boat but there was no help at hand, the Rhyl lifeboat being on its way to help the same Brig as the Point of Air lifeboat.

For over an hour onlookers watched the three men clinging to the side of the boat until all their strength was drained. They then slid quietly into the icy waters and were no more. The tragedy struck into the hearts and minds of every person in the area and much farther afield, and the princely sum of £3,025.19.0d was raised by public donation.

The Docks Board held an official enquiry and evidence was given to the effect that the boat was in perfect condition and did not contribute to the loss of life. It was recorded that the crew was not wearing life jackets for the reason that every man hated the heavy cork. The Board directed however that, henceforth, anyone seen in a lifeboat without his cork life jacket would be severely fined. The bodies were laid to rest in Llanasa Church and Captain Beck and Mate Sherlack received posthumous awards for their bravery.

The Point of Air lifeboat was maintained until 1923 when, after the introduction of motorised boats, the station was closed. The Hilbre station also closed in 1926.

After Point of Air lifeboat station closed, rescue on the Dee was left to unspecialised craft. The nearest fully rigged lifeboat was at Rhyl, which caused a problem at low tide. A tractor took up to twenty-five minutes to launch the boat across the sands, and the Foryd harbour was of little help since a large boat would not float at low water. But a horrific loss at Fflint on Boxing Night 1957 was to change all this.

Tom Bithell was a local shopkeeper, but came from a long line of seafarers and fishermen. He remembers the night only too well. It was bitterly cold and someone was in trouble off the notorious Crosville Point and local people and police officers went to assist.

\* \* \*

We ran to some small boats that were tied on the foreshore, but all the diesel engines were frozen, rendering them useless. So everyone plodded through the pitch darkness to the shore, but the howling wind was playing tricks with the man's muted cries. Then, when we were right out on the sands the wind suddenly fell and a pea soup like fog enveloped us, blotting out the stranded man's calls as well as ours.

We froze in our clothes as the fog thickened, and nearly became victims ourselves. Someone produced a compass and by linking hands we tried to head for the shoreline.

Against our advice, Sergeant Jones of Fflint Police went up to his neck into the water in a desperate last attempt to find the man. We somehow managed to retrieve the Sergeant, covered in ice, and then stood in the freezing fog listening to the doomed man. His cries became weaker and weaker until a gripping silence graphically spelt the end.

We were all very upset by what had happened but managed to return, hand in hand, through the fog across the marsh. It was swirling first one way and then the other and we couldn't even see our footprints in the silt. I can tell you that there isn't an estuary in the country as dangerous as this one.

Inspector Brynmor Roberts of Fflint Police arrived at my shop the next day, in a distressed state. He was a hardened, experienced police officer, but the cries of the trapped man, and the gripping silence that followed, had shaken even him. He had decided that we needed a lifeboat and we set about raising the necessary money.

There followed a series of raffles, collections, dances and all manner of fund-raising events and the sum of £365 was realised to buy a boat with a small 1½-hp engine. Peter Bithell, a relative of mine, was a fisherman and lived on the foreshore. He cleared a small shed of nets, anchors and all sorts of accumulated junk and this is where the boat was kept. The shed leaked badly but it was better than nothing, and Peter lived close enough to ensure that the engine never froze.

The boat was named after C E M Edwards who was then Mayor of Fflint. The Vicar blessed it at a special service one Sunday morning, and that very Sunday afternoon it was called out to save three German women who had attempted to cross the estuary on foot from Neston, without considering the tide. Brynmor Roberts towed the boat behind his car at full speed to the launching area at Bagillt. The three rather wet ladies were saved and we all breathed a sigh of relief. The little boat had got off the mark in saving three lives that would otherwise have probably been lost.

Early in 1961 the boat was called out to rescue three small children that were marooned on mudflats in the estuary. The crew of two was Peter and myself. We crossed what water there was, having to drag the boat over sand to the next water and all the time we could see that the tide was coming up. We never thought we could get to them in time, but we did it somehow. You've never seen three more exhausted little mites in your life.

In the same year, a wild fowler got into quicksand off Oakenholt Papermills. It was a very close thing. As we approached him, we could see his gun above his head with just his head sticking above the gurgling sands. He was going fast. His dog was on the dry sand nearby jumping up and down having a marvellous time thinking it was all fun. We got the man into the boat and to the shore. The bugger jumped out of the boat and went off into the sunset without even a thank-you.

It got that you couldn't move far in the end. It was almost a full-time job, with someone in trouble somewhere all the time. Whether people became foolhardy because we had the boat I don't know, but we certainly worked hard.

But we were not always successful. One time the engine had broken down and was away being repaired. A call came through that three men had attempted to walk from Neston across the sands and, as usual, they had not taken the tides into account and were cut-off. They launched the boat but had to row into a terrible wind. The two-man crew rowed all they could but wrestling against that wind and a rising tide was too much. The tide rose around the men and the rowers shouted to raise their spirits, but by the time they were reached they had collapsed with exhaustion and drowned. If only that blasted engine had been there, they would have been brought safe and well to Fflint.

\* \* \*

In 1966 the lifeboat was taken over by the RNLI and £18,000 was raised for a new lifeboat station. Unable to employ a builder the crew built it themselves and a new inflatable boat arrived, which was lighter to pull over the sandbanks. The new equipment included weatherproof clothing for the crew.

Today, there is an updated inflatable boat at Fflint, complete with a powerful tractor for towing across the mud flats at low water. The secretary now is the quiet spoken Gary Jones.

\* \* \*

We turn out on average about twenty times a year and have saved over fifty lives on the Dee since the new boat arrived. Obviously not all of them are up to their necks in mud. We pick up sick and injured seamen from ships using Mostyn and British Steel docks. Then there are small boats with engine failure or those walkers and wild fowlers who are stupid to forget about the tide. It's never still on this estuary I can tell you.

One night in 1985 two fishermen had placed stake-nets out on the English side of the estuary. After finishing their chores, one of them got into trouble and the other one went for help. It was a hell of a night. A fog fell like lead, it was raining heavily and windy and there was a tide belting up the estuary. The Devil himself couldn't have come up with worse conditions. I stood on the mud flats firing *Paraflares* into the sky in the hope that we might get a direction on the man. We could hear his muffled cries but couldn't decide where they came from.

After fourteen flares had gone off the man was found chest-deep in silt and he was pulled free. One of the crew, Alan Forrester rolled onto his back and slowly edged the man, in a collapsed state, free of the quicksand. It was a hell of a feat. That chappie was within seconds of going under and Alan had to watch his step in case he was also pulled down. The man was in a very poor state when we got him back in the boat.

Alan Forrester received the Humane Society Award for his work that night, but this was not Alan's first award by any means, or the crew's. On Saturday February 26, 1983, several 999 calls were received following a call for help on a citizen band radio from the crew of *Heron 11*, a boat that was in trouble one mile south of Mostyn docks. In a strong, freezing Force 5-6 the inflatable was launched from Fflint and we knew that there was less than two hours before the tide flooded. Visibility was poor and getting worse. The weather was so bad that I had to think twice about ordering the launch of our boat. It was over the limit really for when a 'D' class inflatable could be safely launched. But if I had withdrawn the order, which I had the power to do, there would have been a mutiny among the lads. Weather and conditions don't matter to them at all.

On arriving at the groyne at Mostyn I fired a Paraflare to warn the crew of *Heron 11*, who responded by flashing a torch. Alan Forrester was at the helm and even he was concerned at the dock mouth when they faced waves of over six-foot. With a coolness that comes only from experience and a certain type of man, he steered the boat with split-second timing through the waves.

They soon saw the stricken boat with anchors out and waves crashing over her. The wind was now Force 8 and increasing and a flood tide was running at over four knots. It was impossible to make a line fast for a tow so Forrester decided to take off the crew. It took several attempts to get alongside and when they did one of the crew was collapsed in terror and cold. Eventually the *Heron* crew were lifted into the lifeboat and Smith, one of the lifeboat crew, had to lie across the casualty to retain him in the boat as it was buffeted by a gale that was now out of all proportion to the size of our boat.

Forrester knew that it would be impossible to land at Mostyn but the only other suitable place to land was six miles down river and the chances of making it were not good. So he tried again for Mostyn taking more than ten minutes to breach the waves, which were now well over seven feet high, and travel 300 yards to the beach. This was eventually achieved and the casualties were safely landed. *Heron 11* sank thirty minutes after they left her.

* * *

Alan Forrester received a Bronze award for his bravery, as well as framed letters from the Duke of Atholl, the president of the RNLI. Crewmen Dennis Smith and Terrence Jacklin were also awarded honours.

These accounts are just a few of the many lives that have been saved by lifeboats on both sides of the estuary. As Sod's law dictates, boats do have engine failures and wild fowlers do get trapped – and it's rare for this to happen in ninety-degree heat, and in windless conditions.

There is no longer a trace of the Point of Air lifeboat station. They were buried by the sands of Talacre Warren, rather than demolished. Tourists come to Talacre today to see the lighthouse and to bake among the sand dunes, which shield the breeze off the seas. There are caravans there, although the beach is not as good as Prestatyn a little further up the coast where the sand is softer. An added bonus is the absence of the quicksand that blights the Talacre coast.

The increasing height of the sea and the increasing ferocity of the winter gales mean that land around here is being lost to the sea. To counteract this, nature conservancy and local wildlife trusts have embarked on a huge dune protection scheme at Talacre. Dunes have been fenced off and old Christmas trees have been planted in the sand in an effort to encourage Maram grasses to knit together and support the dunes, in defence against flooding. Provided that ignorant (as yet) motor bike scramblers and mountain-bikers stay away from the dunes as requested, there is a chance that the defence may work and that the all important dunes may survive. But they must be left alone. Gales during the winters of the late 1980s swept away an entire row of dunes, some of them up to twenty or more feet high, giving less defence to the next row of dunes, which have a precarious lifeline as it is. Add to this the pressure on the remaining dunes from human feet, motorcycles and mountain bikes and the problem is hugely compounded. The consequences to those that live and farm in the shade of the dunes are dire should the seas break through as they did prior to the 18th century. Those with biblical knowledge will tell you that the sea always claims back what is rightfully hers. Certainly on the coastal strip from Prestatyn to Fflint the sea is in a reclaiming mood and, on present evidence, she might just win.

Visitors to Talacre will see that the paths through the dunes are clearly sign-posted, and that they are requested to comply with the conservation measures and stay on the paths. On the right of the car park is a clearly sign-posted area that is marked out as a nature reserve. This is especially important for the millions of incoming flocks of birds that winter in Wales. It is well worth a visit with a pair of binoculars, and wellington boots are a definite investment because the base is rather more silt and mud than sand as each tide fetches-up more silt, some of it probably containing human waste deposited out at sea.

Since the departure of the local fibre-factories and some chemical industries, the cockles have returned in vast numbers and the E.A. is now moving to protect these shellfish from exploitation. We can only assume that the discharges that have now ceased – and which never officially existed– have cleaned up this part of the Dee, or God help those who eat cockles.

Anyone can collect cockles, which is where the problem lies. Cockles are easy to catch, because they lie just below the surface and stay dormant until the tide returns. They eat by sifting through the current that flows over them, containing micro-particles of food. This rather boring lifestyle could be their own undoing since the cockle beds at Talacre are being hammered. Environment Agency is moving to protect cockles, but they might be too late. This is a haven for the fast-buck 'Dole Dodgers' who have recently moved on to these flats by the score to harvest the shellfish for an illegal export market. There have been many bloody conflicts between them and customs-men, department of health officials and tax inspectors.

I was totally unaware of their existence a few years ago when walking across the beach to photograph the lighthouse. There was a flat-back lorry with its number-plates removed and twenty or more youths and men, some with face-masks, loading sacks from quad-bikes on to the lorry. Completely ignorant of the situation, I was approached but managed to convince them during a heated exchange that I was not from the tax or dole-office, but a bona-fide photographer seeking some snaps of the lighthouse on an incoming tide.

People later advised me that a dole-officer had been hospitalised through meeting a pickaxe handle wielded by a hooded man who was never identified. I was lucky, but this story ties in nicely with the history of smuggling on this warren in by gone days. Time may have moved on but some things never change. The quad-bike might be a modern addition to an old trade that is carried out by men with hidden faces, who still prefer to use the cover of darkness.

# The Case of the Salmon of the River Dee

Salmon have been netted in the Dee estuary throughout history and prehistory. The present regulations governing netting are by-laws from the 19th century, and they have changed little since then.

The salmon stock, however, is far lower today than it has ever been. The first sign of enormous depletion was a deadly virus in 1967 from which the Dee stocks failed to recover. This has been compounded by the policy regarding the netting of salmon and sea trout off the Irish coast. The Irish refuse to see sense on salmon stocks, regarding them as an inexhaustible supply of food, and most attempts by the British Government to get more tolerant netting quotas fall on deaf ears.

Britain's plans to halt the decline include removing many nets from estuaries and placing stricter controls on those that remain. A trapping station was erected to tag fish at Chester so as to monitor the movement of fish over the weir in fresh water and in estuarine water below Chester Weir. Fees were paid to anglers or netsmen who (legally) caught a tagged salmon and the full details of the life history of the fish were sent to its captor. It was an excellent opportunity for all participants to become actively involved and data collated from tagging gave the scientists a fairer idea of what was going on. The Environmental Agency has not verified stories of stressed fish dying within days of being tagged but they could well be true to some extent.

In November 1996 the proposals of the Environmental Agency (or National Rivers Authority as it was then) were called to account at Chester Guildhall by netsmen who opposed the reduction of netting below Chester Weir and the Cop (where the old port of Chester once stood). The Public Enquiry was a lively affair with anglers on one side and netsmen on the other, and the Environmental Agency sitting uncomfortably in the middle. There was a precedent in that Scottish salmon rivers had already been through this process, and their experiences had to be considered.

The crux of the problem in Scotland lay in excessive netting operations where perhaps two-thirds of the fish were taken by nets, leaving a miserable one third to rod and line and to breed. Numbers were therefore insufficient for a breeding programme that would safeguard future salmon stocks. Anglers consorted with landowners and various other bodies and the nets were 'bought-off' the estuaries. Initial reaction was favourable as the salmon stocks increased considerably for angling, and more fish were able to breed. This caused unseen land agents to approach the riparian landowners, and they pointed out that the time was ripe to cash-in. The owners agreed.

Many fishing rights were withdrawn or not renewed and the right to fish for salmon was sold to the highest bidder. The buyers were often from Japan, Arabia or America, and local people suddenly found themselves with bills for thousands of pounds to fish local salmon. The owners knew that the local anglers had been priced out, but financial priorities superseded the moral ones.

There was an argument throughout the enquiry that several landowners in the Welsh Dee valley would do exactly the same. Locals would be denied access to reasonably priced salmon fishing, as would visitors who were so important in supporting the local economy. There was a definite requirement to reduce netting so as to preserve salmon stocks for future generations, but there had to be a sensible balance between nets and rods on the estuary.

Netting serves several purposes. If catches are properly documented it gives some idea of the number of fish passing through the estuary, adding to data gathered from the trap at Chester, which only catches a small percentage of fish and is therefore only a guide. Salmon is also an important source of food and revenue that should be harvested under strict control by both rod and net.

But it was obvious from the returns of the nets that most catches were under documented because a net licence cost almost £400 per season, and average returns were less than £100 per season. Having been involved in covert operations to estimate the reality of netting on the area adjacent to Chester race-course, the netsmen were openly talking of catches of fifty fish per netting session. Given an average of 10lbs weight per fish this makes a total of £1,000 per tide if the fish retail at a very conservative £2 per pound to a wholesaler, or more to a local hotel. Most netsmen were receiving £2.50 and more per pound following the contamination scare of farmed Scottish salmon, when it was revealed that chemicals were added to make the flesh pink in the farmed species. Yet, the official financial returns of the nets showed less than £100 *per season* for fish sold. It was farcical and had to be controlled.

Reference was made to the seals in the estuary, and in particular to Hoyle Bank where they lie-up at low water (usually 200-250 in number). It was also noted that seals were frequently seen at Chester Weir. Reference was also made that fish were caught with seal scratches or injuries on them, and this was a further relevant factor in the decline of stocks. The Cormorant population at Chester Weir was also mentioned as taking smolt (immature salmon going out to sea to mature from the higher reaches of the Dee), this being seen as another possible factor having a detrimental effect on fish stocks. The enquiry and the NRA acknowledged both factors, but there is much work to be done culling could be justified.

The NRA, as it then was, applied to reduce the nets from thirty overall to sixteen (eight above Queensferry Bridge and eight below), and to reduce the trammel nets from four to two, with the uppermost region for salmon and sea-trout netting to be Cop Point. The enquiry agreed.

The question of water abstraction was also mentioned as a realistic problem for migratory fish leaving the tidal zone and coming up river to reproduce. But the NRA was a little barren in its support on this sensitive area of complaint.

Owners of pleasure boats operating above Chester Weir have complained for a long time that boats are grounding in lowering water levels, and their undersides are subsequently being damaged. This is a direct result of the reduced flow being insufficient to send the silt out over the weir to sea. Less rain in the upper regions has also resulted in the Dee actually slowing down as it travels seaward, and the silt it used to remove now lies on the bed. Spawning areas have been subsequently destroyed in the higher reaches. Another effect of the increased silting on the estuarine beats is that the tidal bore, for which the Dee was once famous, has all but stopped. It was a monthly spectacle in days gone-by but has now abated to almost nothing.

The reduction in the number of nets and a shorter netting season took effect from 1997 and is already showing great benefits. But it will do little good if international fishing laws are not changed to govern salmon trawling on the high seas and coastal netting operations elsewhere. Hopefully then the magnificent sight of salmon leaping the weir will be not confined to old film footage.

Fishing with rod and line is a case of 99% luck and 1% skill. You can have several salmon in a pool in a river and not one single fish will take the bait, perhaps for days on end, perhaps forever. But there is no luck for a salmon trapped in a pool at low water, where they are easily picked off by a net. This reduces the overall number of fish taken by rod and line, but more importantly reduces the number of fish pass the angler to arrive at traditional spawning grounds many miles upstream, which is the only way to ensure the survival of the species. Conservation is paramount in the present climate. It is a crop that should be harvested yes, but common sense must prevail. Yesterday's greed has caused today's shortage. This is the reality of the declining salmon stocks in the Welsh Dee as it is in many other rivers all over the world.

## To the Future

Through the chapters of this book we have seen the rise and fall of the Dee estuary as a shipping force. We know that the changes in ship sizes could never be accommodated today, by the river let alone by the little ports. There are bigger private yachts on the seas of the world today than the biggest ships of yesteryear on the Dee.

But whereas the ships keep away, the wild birds do not and the Dee estuary is now accepted as being the most important estuary for wintering birds anywhere in Britain. It is not a good breeding site, but in wintertime the numbers of birds on the estuary increase by over 500%, and each winter new and more numerous species arrive. The RSPB is now a major landowner on the estuary with many thousands of estuary acres preserved for the birds to give them rich winter feeding grounds in the silt. Ironically the very silt that closed the Dee to ships is attracting the birds by the thousand. Dee wild fowlers are working closely with the RSPB to ensure that the birds are not unduly harassed, and they are releasing large numbers of birds for sport, a move that is indeed applauded by the RSPB.

In the centre of the estuary at low water there is a massive sandbank known as the 'Hoyle Bank', which is roughly one mile long by two miles across. This is a resting-place for an ever-increasing number of common and grey seals. They do not breed here but spend most of the summer in numbers often in excess of two hundred and fifty mammals. Councils on the Wirral have licensed boats to carry twelve passengers or more to see the seals on Hoyle Bank at low water, and many people come to study its wildlife. The income is much appreciated by the fishermen in view of their flagging livelihood.

The estuary has also been designated a Site of Specific Scientific Interest (SSSI) by the Government, which should afford special protection to most of its wildlife. Whether it does in reality remains to be seen.

Part of the estuary is also zoned off as a special Bass nursery area and all fishing within the zone is forbidden to protect the Bass, which as a slow growing species is struggling for survival on many estuaries. This move by the Environment Agency has been warmly welcomed by conservationists, but has had a cool reception from commercial fishermen. The Allis Shad, another sea-going fish that is now fully protected and almost extinct in many rivers, appears to be on the way back in the Dee which is a positive sign for conservation and an indication of the improved attitude since the NRA/Environment Agency was founded.

The estuary however is far from being a site of utter tranquillity and peace. The seals on the Hoyle Bank began dying in fairly large numbers in 1989 and post mortems officially declared that they were suffering from 'a virus'. Seals were also dying on the east coast of England off Norfolk at that time, but scientists stated that the Norfolk coast 'virus' was different to the Hoyle Bank virus. But many thought that it much more sinister than this.

Greenpeace made public some disturbing findings within the estuary. Blood samples taken from eels and seals demonstrated that the Dee estuary and Liverpool Bay (which is in effect an extension of the same stretch of water) had the highest levels of PCB's, Dieldrin and Mercury found in any British estuary. There is also great concern at the increased ulceration on flatfish within the estuary. Flatfish have a certain amount of natural ulceration, but the amount of fish caught and thrown back because they are unsaleable far exceeds any natural state. Environmental Agency scientists have not acknowledged the findings but conservationists are very worried.

Salmon are now recovering since the Environment Agency reduced the amount of netting on the estuary, but international measures are still needed to safeguard the species' survival. The delicate cockle and mussel beds are also under pressure and much more attention will have to be given to safeguard their fragile existence. Seafood should be a matter of great public concern in this new century.

So where is all this pollution coming from? Well, very little is actually tipped into the sea illegally. Most of the chemicals tipped there come from firms with household names like ICI, La Porte, Unichem Chemicals, Shell Petrol, Unilever, Van Den Burgs & Jurgens and many more. The companies tip chemicals into the estuary by Government decree, either from a boat or through effluent pipes. Add to this the millions of gallons of raw-sewage that local water authorities still tip into the sea, although drastic measures are being taken to reduce this practise. The Nuclear

Power industry has huge installations in Cumbria and on Anglesey, all adding to the radioactivity of the seas. Yet, despite overwhelming evidence from Greenpeace and many other recognised authorities, the tipping goes on.

The old Connah's Quay coal-fired power station has now been demolished and replaced by a gas-fired power station. Alongside the power station is the third crossing of the Dee, which has been dubbed by critics as 'the road to nowhere'. It was supposed to relieved traffic congestion on Deeside, but in reality the opposite seems to be the case. Arguments still rage for and against a Fflint by-pass, which would be built across the marshes to the front of Fflint castle. A public enquiry was held and thankfully the Inspector came firmly down against the plan, but rumblings still continue.

The new menaces on the estuarine beats are noisy water-skiers and ignorant jet-skiers. Fishermen claim that due to the high speeds at which they travel the back-wash causes their fishing boats to rise and fall violently whilst at anchor, damaging the boat bottoms and hulls. In turn, the skiers claim that the netsmen pay out the nets in front of them as they approach, causing collisions, injury and damage.

But the main threat to the estuary is that of over industrialisation. The expanse of industry on Deeside is phenomenal and if unchecked will soon swallow up the entire estuary. Relatively cheap land and a willing workforce make expansion very viable, but at what price to the estuary and its wildlife?

# Appendix I

## Extracts from the Mostyn Estate Ports Book

March 17th 1757      Part of the wreckage of a ship came ashore at Talacre with six men still clinging to it. Sixteen lives lost.

January 19th 1759      Sold a Dale-Mast to Thomas Powell, a boatman from Mostyn on behalf of Mr Goodwin, a merchant from Chester for £2.10.0d

June 11th 1760      Robert Griffiths of Whitford drowned whilst bathing at Fflint. The body when found had a rope around its middle. The tide took the body away from Thomas Hale and went out to sea and was fetched up at Point of Air on June 13th to be recovered by the parishioners of Whitford.

September 4th 1760      A Brig from Dublin to Liverpool came ashore on a night-tide at Point of Air. Captain was Pilling-Lawson and the ship owned by Mr Law-Smith & Sons. The vessel was refloated on September 10th 1760 and went to Parkgate for repair.

July 24th 1762      A boat that was wrecked at sea came ashore under the 'Star Hills' landmark with both sides burst outwards. With the boat came three sailcloths, one anchor, and a cable with a mast and some ropes. All brought to Talacre. A local man who was on the beach with his horse was paid 2/-d to recover the wreck and to take it into the care of the Mostyn estate

July 20th 1763      On a night of intense gales two ships came ashore near Talacre. One of 25 tons (*Two Brothers*) was bound for Chester from Red Wharf Bay on Anglesey. The other was a 16-ton ship called *Providence*. Both were carrying wines and other valuables. Both foundered with a loss of over 100 lives between them.

| | |
|---|---|
| Autumn 1763 | Barrels of herring washed-up at Talacre. They were distributed among the locals for the sum of six pence per hundred. |
| November 13th 1765 | Casks of tar came ashore at Towyn and as they were not claimed, Sir Piers Mostyn put them to his own use. |
| November 13th 1765 | A fishing boat belonging to Thomas Price and part-owned by William Roberts from Parkgate came ashore, having gone over by the 'Star Hills' near Towyn, all four hands on board drowning. |
| November 14th 1765 | Bodies released back to Parkgate after a Coroners Inquest. 5/-d paid for the sum of recovering the bodies. |
| February 5th 1766 | 3/6d paid to Elizabeth Salisbury for the team of horses used to draw a Deal mast ashore. |
| November 9th 1770 | Five men perished in a small boat that they used following the wrecking of a pilot-boat near Hilbre. |
| December 9th 1770 | Goods including butter and trunks of clothing came ashore with a hogshead of tallow following a ship foundering off Hoylake Roads in the Liverpool Channel. Boat owned by a Mr Bevan of Aston, Lancashire. All on board drowned. |
| March 10th 1771 | Body of a man came ashore. |
| March 17th 1771 | Body of a woman came ashore. 5/-d paid to John Harvey for two graves. 16/- paid for two coffins. 4/-d paid for ale-money for all concerned with burials. 1/3d paid to Thomas Stanley to go to Mold to inform the Coroner by letter. |
| October 6th 1775 | Large Brig grounded at Point of Air, en-route from France to Liverpool. Within two tides, 'country |

people' had cut her to pieces and stole a great deal of timber.

Many people arrested and taken to St Asaph prison and detained there until the next Assize Court. (Trial sent many local people Fflint gaol for lengthy terms.) It cost £6.5.4d to incarcerate these people and a further £8.7.10d for the wreck to be removed.

(Considering the smuggling of French goods on this coast, it seems extremely harsh treatment of the 'country people' especially when the complainant was so prominent in smuggling operations.)

October 24th 1775     Three bodies found at Talacre. Cost of coffins and burials £2.2.4d. A long boat also recovered.

November 22nd 1776 Two men and a woman found drowned at Talacre and they had almost £30 on their bodies.

January 1st 1779     *Les Deux a Mis* wrecked off Mostyn in a gale. She carried silks, calicos, cushions, china, japan ware, tea, coffee, wire and cones. Much was recovered and a great deal was stolen by the 'local people'. Sir Piers Mostyn did little as the wreck was nearer Mostyn than Talacre. Between 30-40 lives were lost and they were buried without coffins. The merchants had overall control of the dead and Sir Piers Mostyn was most unhappy when he discovered the facts and stated that had he known he would have paid for coffins himself.

August 30th 1780     The body of a man fetched-up at Point of Air under the lighthouse. The ½d found on him was given to the man who went for the Coroner.

November 9th 1781     Brig stranded under Talacre, laden with herrings. She was unloaded to be repaired, and the load guarded. She got away on December 12, 1781 but her cargo was ruined.

| | |
|---|---|
| August 8th 1783 | The body of a man found on the beach and buried at Llanasaph. The cost of fetching the Coroner was 1/4d. |
| April 22nd 1785 | A corpse found by The Warren House at Talacre. The Coroner was sent for and on the 24th the mother of the corpse, Mrs Jane Hughes of Rhuddlan, took the body home in a coffin donated by Sir Piers Mostyn. |
| November 7th 1785 | Ship (*S. Batchelor*) wrecked during the night in a severe gale. |
| November 30th 1786 | *The Hawk Packet* of Liverpool came ashore between The Warren House and the lighthouse. Later in the night 10 sloops grounded but the weather improved and they all got away. |
| March 11th 1790 | The body of a man came ashore and was taken home to Liverpool by his father. Two miners called Francis Brooke and Thomas Wyre found the body. |
| December 15th 1790 | A vessel called *Newbern of Newbern* from North Carolina bound for Glasgow port and commanded by John Scott, was wrecked. The captain, cook and a young gentleman passenger perished in the cold. She had a cargo of tar, pitch, turnips, staves, and wooden-planks. |
| January 20th 1791 | Fierce gales – the worst for 20 years. More damage caused to shipping than was ever known. Brig and sloop driven ashore in the night and a sloop went down at Mostyn Deeps but the crew saved same night. |
| February 13th 1791 | A sloop *The Friendship* from Arundel in Essex bound for Liverpool, full of barley, wrecked between the lighthouse and The Warren House. One male corpse recovered the next day. |

| | |
|---|---|
| July 1st 1793 | The body of a man found on the shore at Morfa and the Coroner sent for from Mold. He was unable to come as he had another to attend to and ordered that the burial go ahead at Llanasa without the need for a jury. |
| January 29th 1794 | A vessel foundered near Talacre lighthouse. Between the vessel coming ashore and the teams arriving with horses, the ship was taken to bits and such cargo as was left was not worth recovering. (Those locals at it again.) |
| November 15th 1797 | The body of John Christian Curwen left by the tide near Point of Air. |
| November 20th 1797 | The Brig *John*, under Captain John Moleyneaux from Liverpool, wrecked by Point of Air lighthouse. He was drowned and friends buried him at Llanasa. |
| January 4th 1802 | Bill for wreckage recovered from Point of Air to a Mr Sleight: |

| | |
|---|---|
| 4 boats | £10.10.0d |
| 5 beams | 2.12.6d |
| Waste | 10.6d |
| Mast & bowsprit | 2. 1.5d |
| Cabelling | 6. 6.0d |
| 2 booms | 9.0d |
| 2 sails | 2.15.0d |
| Anchor | 3. 2.6d |

| | |
|---|---|
| January 7th 1806 | Headless body of a female found at the lighthouse at Point of Air. It was in a very poor condition. |
| January 10th 1806 | *Teleaman* from Liverpool bound for the West Indies stranded at the lighthouse after a severe gale blew for two days. The ship broke-up and 19 boys and 8 men perished. Most of the bodies stayed on the Lancashire side of the estuary. Bainbridge, Horsfall & Co. Ltd from Liverpool owned the ship. |

March 21st 1806    Unidentified body of a man washed ashore below
                   Gwespyr in the marshes. All the flesh eaten away
                   from the face. He was supposed to be the mate of
                   the *Hopewell of Holyhead* that sank off Abergele full
                   of tanned leather bound for Liverpool. Two boys
                   and the Captain were not found.

June 22nd 1806     Woman washed ashore, and was supposed to be
                   the companion of the woman found on 7.1.06. The
                   body was almost rotted away and is thought to be
                   part of a party of 3 men and 2 women who were
                   coal-traders from Anglesey.

November 22nd 1807 Ship came ashore at Point of Air lighthouse
                   carrying timber.

September 6th 1809 The body of an eleven year old boy found by the
                   Point of Air lighthouse. The boy had been lost
                   whilst fishing with his father who also drowned
                   near Beaumaris. He was William Jones and his
                   father Richard Jones was found on the foreshore by
                   Foryd (Rhyl). They came from Parkgate and were
                   buried at Dyserth. The wife and mother was left
                   with five children.

September 2nd 1822 Severe gales all night. Vessel *The Victory Alexander
                   Morrison* mounted with 18 carriage guns bound
                   from Liverpool to Africa, was wrecked off Isle
                   Sands. Little found of the wreck.

Other entries from the Mostyn estate book include:

The *King George*, a steamer went down off Salisbury Bank in 1807
during a severe gale with the loss of over 100 Irish labourers and the
crew. Another notable wreck was *Lelia*, a 640 ton paddle steamer / cutter
that left Liverpool on January 14th 1865 in abnormally high seas. She
sank with her cargo of 750 tons of coal off Prestatyn, and the Pilot still on
board. Captain Skinner also died. Two boats with thirty men got away.
They were later thrown into the sea made it to the lighthouse and clung
to it for forty-eight hours until the gale ceased. The Captain's body was
recovered some time later in a fishing-net and his watch had stopped at
4.10pm, the time the *Lelia* sank. Evidence was given to the enquiry to the

effect that the Captain wished to stay ashore until the storm abated but he was under instructions from the ship's owners to put to sea despite the severity of the gale.

Sometime in 1897 the *Trekieve* went aground just off Mostyn as she tried a hasty entry into Mostyn docks. She was carrying iron ore and broke up. Those dreadful 'local people' arrived and looted what was left of the ship, taking away what the sea had not claimed. Another famous and well-known wreck is the *Barron Hill*, which went down in 1934 carrying lead from Fflint. She was never floated again and markers now light her wreck.

Also in 1934 the *Santa Rosa* went on fire in Point of Air dock laden with coal. She blocked the harbour for some time until moved. There is no mention of any loss of life.

*Lord Delamere* grounded in the channel off Connah's Quay. It was this wreck, with its mast protruding above the sea, which was the reason for this book. The mast was blown-up in 1987 as the channel had shifted again, and she caused a danger to ships entering Summers Wharf at the steelworks. She was carrying grain for the local brewery, to the old tie-up at Rockcliffe Hall just above Connah's Quay. Within two tides of her grounding, she was so fast that she never moved again.

World War II also took its toll of ships on the Dee Estuary. One ship from Liverpool took a trip to Mostyn against all advice and hit one of our own mines in 1940. All lives on board were lost. An unnamed ship apparently hit a floating mine in the estuary mouth and sank, again with a loss of life in 1940.

*Cambourne* was a ship, owned by a Captain Shaw, plying between the Dee and Ireland in the 1920's. She was fitted with a diesel engine as well as sail. Lying off Limerick she came under crossfire whilst at the quayside and when she returned to Chester, the bullet-holes in her bodywork were a centre of much attraction. Captain Shaw told vivid accounts of sea-monsters near Limerick that had been witnessed by both crew and bystanders on the quayside.

In 1936 the Government chartered the ship to take troops to County Cork. Whilst on one trip the winds reached 108 mph, blowing her out into the Atlantic. She was out there for four days but returned safely with no loss of life.

# Appendix II

## Ships of the Chester River

The days of Topsail Schooners and Clippers sailing the Dee tide may have gone for ever, but here are some of the names that small boys might have collected before train engines became such an obsession.

| | |
|---|---|
| *Agenaia* | Two-mast topsail schooner built 1879 by Duncan of Kingston. Gross tonnage 145 tons. Wrecked off Guernsey, May 1913. |
| *Agnes Craig* | Built as a three-mast topsail schooner by Ferguson & Baird at Connah's Quay in 1884. Weight of 128 tons. She later changed her name to *Irish Marie* and was broken up in Arklow in 1952. |
| *Alexandra* | Two-mast ketch built in Poole in 1891. Reney, the sailmaker of Connah's Quay, later bought her. She was sold to Beaumaris in 1890. |
| *Alfred* | Two-mast topsail schooner of 48 tons bought by Reney of Connah's Quay. |
| *Alfred* | Two-mast topsail schooner built at Fflint 1865 and registered at Padstow. |
| *Alice Linda* | She was 85 tons gross weight, bought by Coppacks of Connah's Quay and registered at Chester. She sank off Mostyn Deep in 1913 whilst at anchor, with Captain J Garratt asleep in his bunk below deck. The mate Ned Hughes was saved and divers later recovered the body of Captain Garratt. |
| *Ann* | Sloop of 26 tons registered at Beaumaris. She was built at Conwy and bought by Robert Edwards of Connah's Quay in the early 1860s. Part of her log book shows: |

March 7 1863  Greenfield to Liverpool – gunpowder
March 9 1863  Liverpool to Greenfield – wheat

March 20 1863 Greenfield to Liverpool – turnips
March 27 1863 Liverpool to Greenfield – wheat
April 21 1863  Liverpool to Greenfield – zinc

**Anna Maria**

A two-mast topsail schooner built at Queensferry in 1837. She was lost in the Bristol Channel in 1859 in a storm.

**Annie Brocklebank**

A three-mast topsail schooner of 120 tons built in 1869 at Ulverston. Owned by Reney the sailmaker of Connah's Quay. Her last Captain was R M Williams, he was lost with his ship on Hazleborough Sands in March 1914, whilst on a voyage to Newcastle.

**Annie Jones**

A two-mast schooner built at Rhyl in 1892. She was 77 tons and last owned by Vickers of Connah's Quay.

**Baltic**

A two-mast topsail schooner of 87 tons built by Jones of Rhyl in 1857. She was principally a slate trader and sailed the deep water for many years. She was sold to Ireland and traded the west coast ports. In September 1928 she ran aground and was lost at Rasconberry.

**Beatrice**

A two-mast topsail schooner of 104 tons. Built in 1869 at Barrow. She ceased to operate in 1901.

**Bessie Arnold**

A two-mast topsail schooner of 129 tons built in 1872 by Ferguson & Baird. She was lost in 1875.

**Betsy**

A one mast sloop of 42 tons. She was built at Chester in 1856 and lost in 1875.

**Bidsie & Bell**

A two-mast topsail schooner built in 1869. She was registered at Goole (188 tons) and was later converted to a three-mast for Coppacks of Connah's Quay.

**Balham**

Built as an auxiliary engine ketch at Rye in Sussex at 158 tons. She was a 'Q' ship in the First World War

178

and had one submarine to her credit. Bought by Coppacks in 1937, she was broken up in the docks at Connah's Quay in June 1957.

British Oak      A two-mast schooner built at Chester 1855. She was owned by Bishton of Chester and weighed 78 tons. Lost in 1876.

C S Atkinson      Built at Carrigfergus in 1878 and registered at Belfast. She was owned by Roberts of Bangor and registered again at Chester in 1904. She was further registered at Belfast in 1908. Sadly she was run-down in the English Channel. Her weight was 96 tons.

Caboceer      A two-mast schooner built as a Brig in 1863 by Davison of Liverpool at 108 tons. In 1865 she was sold to Lewis & Co of Mostyn. In 1883 Coppacks bought her and in March 1890 she was stranded off Spain and became a total loss.

Caerwys Castle      Built at Fflint by Jones in 1861 and registered at Chester. She was lost on a run from the Isle of Man to Saltney.

Cambourne      Three-mast double topsail schooner of 118 tons. Built in Amlwch in 1884 by W C Paynter. In 1922 she was owned by a Captain W H Shaw of Arlington and used by him in the Irish coast trade. She was also fitted with an 80hp semi-diesel engine. Bullets struck by when she was lying off Limerick Quay. When the fighting ceased the Government chartered her to take troops to Cork. She was on passage from Gloucester to Tralee in February 1936 when the wind reached 108 mph. and blew her out into the Atlantic. She reached landfour days late. She was sold in 1946.

In his unpublished autobiography Captain Shaw tells of the sea monster he saw in the Shannon Estuary whilst at berth at Limerick. The creature was seen by the crew and by a crowd of people lining the Limerick Quay. It had a long serpent like neck, a small head and a hump on its back. When it swam in line with a yacht, its head reached halfway up the topmast and its hump halfway up the lower mast.

*Catherine Latham*    Two-mast schooner built at Barrow in 1867. She was transferred to Chester in 1898 and bought by Hancocks of Buckley in 1904. She was lost off Douglas on February 14, 1915.

*Catherine Reney*    Built as a ketch in 1901 by Ferguson & Baird at Connah's Quay for Captain Reney, she was lost on New Year's Eve 1905 with all hands off Donaghdee, Northern Ireland. She was carrying bricks and moulded tiles from Connah's Quay to Belfast when a heavy squall struck her about mid-channel and carried away the greater part of her sail and running gear. She lost power and was swept onto rocks. A breeches buoy was fired across the ship but the line failed to take a grip and fouled up. The body of the Captain (Crofts) was brought home and the rest of the crew was buried in Ireland.

*Celtic*    A three-mast double topsail schooner of 228 tons registered at Beaumaris and built in 1894 as a barque. She was owned by Reney of Connah's Quay and was lost off eastern Scotland.

*Charles Edward*    A two-mast topsail schooner built at Connah's Quay in 1858 for D Ferguson. She was lost off Bardsey Island in August 1865.

*Charlotte*    Ketch built at Chester in 1895.

*Chase*    Schooner built at Connah's Quay 1878. Lost in 1904.

*Chester Trader*    A two-mast sloop of 38 tons. She was built at Fflint in 1857 and taken off the register in 1874.

*City of Chester*    Schooner built 1858 at Chester (70 tons).

| | |
|---|---|
| *Claggan* | Schooner of 64 tons built in 1876 and registered at Barrow. She was said to be the first sailing vessel to be built with a motor. |
| *Clive* | 88 tons. Built at Chester in 1837. |
| *Cyril* | A two-mast schooner built at Fflint in 1857. She was 58 tons and lost in 1894. |
| *Donehurst* | Wooden salvage ship converted to a working ship and later owned by Captain R Parry of 'Donehurst' Chester Road, Flint. |
| *Dee* | A flat of 31 tons built at Chester in 1837. She worked out of Crane Wharf, Chester. |
| *Dispatch* | A two-mast double topsail schooner of 120 tons built in Scotland in 1888. She had a beautiful white painted figurehead. On one voyage from Tralee to Gloucester she was blown 500 miles off course into the Atlantic. The crew was saved from starvation by a passing Dutch fishing vessel. She is now a hulk at Avonmouth docks. |
| *Doon* | Single-mast naked flat boat built at Winsford 1869 and registered at Chester in 1913. She was later owned by a Connah's Quay man and was broken up in 1931. |
| *Donald & Doris* | Three-mast topsail schooner of 142 tons built in 1897 by Paynter of Amlwch. She was a Chester River trader for many years. |
| *Duchess* | A two-mast topsail schooner of 110 tons built at Connah's Quay and registered at Chester. She was the last vessel to be built alongside the old Quay wall. For many years she sailed deep waters and then became a coaster. During a gale in 1936 she was dashed her against the sea wall by a violent gust and became a total loss. |

| | |
|---|---|
| *Earl of Beaconsfield*<br>*(Little)* | Three-mast topsail schooner of 91 tons built by Ferguson & Baird at Connah's Quay. |
| *Earl of Beaconsfield*<br>*(Big)* | 169 tons built at Connah's Quay by Ferguson & Baird in 1903 for Hancocks of Buckley. She was run-down in the Irish Sea between South Rock and Copelands Lighthouse by an Irish cattle boat in 1906. The ship was lost but the crew saved. |
| *Earl Cairns* | A two-mast topsail schooner of 127 tons launched April 1883 by Ferguson & Baird, Hancocks of Buckley later owned her. She traded from Fflint as well as Connah's Quay for a long time. Then she was badly damaged by fire in the Severn and came into the hands of P K Harris of Appledore, who repaired her. She was given an engine and sailed as a fully rigged schooner from Liverpool.<br>At the outbreak of World War II, she was commandeered for barage ballon duties off Falmouth. At the end of the war she was condemned to lay there but it is believed that she was saved and later sold to Newfoundland. |
| *Earl of Latham* | A three-mast topsail schooner of 132 tons, built by Ferguson & Baird at Connah's Quay. Bought by Hancocks of Buckley in 1913, while on a voyage from Connah's Quay to Limerick in 1915 a German submarine that was waiting for the Lusitania (a 31,000-ton monster) sank her in mistake. |
| *Eliza Baird* | Schooner of 60 tons built at Chester in 1856. |
| *Elizabeth Hyam* | A two-mast topsail schooner of 102 tons. Built at Connah's Quay in 1875 by Ferguson & Baird, in 1895 she was owned by Matthais of Connah's Quay. She was lost off Ramsey. |
| *Ellie Park* | A two-mast topsail schooner of 99 tons built in 1879 at Barrow. Later re-rigged at Connah's Quay, she |

was a regular trader on Chester River.

**Emily Barratt**

A two-mast schooner built by Duddon Shipbuilding Company and launched 1913. The last wooden sailing vessel built on the Lancashire coast. After being used for barrage balloons, she was rebuilt in 1947 and became a regular Chester River trader carrying coal for many years.

**Emily Helena**

A two-mast topsail schooner built in Chester 1862. James Reney owned her and she was lost in 1891.

**Emily Millington**

Three-mast topsail schooner of 111 tons built in 1876 at Selby. Thomas & Sons of Amlwch later owned her and she traded regularly to Crane Wharf. One of her masters, Captain Godfrey, fell into Chester dock and drowned.

**Emily Warbrick**

Built as a brig of 16 tons at Fleetwood in 1872 for deep water trading, she was later owned by Reney of Connah's Quay. She was later converted to a three-mast topsail schooner and spent the First World War tied up at Connah's Quay. After the war she was refitted as a cruising yacht and re-named *Lost Horizion*.

**Emma-Ester**

Two-mast schooner of 108 tons built in 1871 at Perth. Owned by Reney of Connah's Quay and carried bricks to Belfast. She went aground on one trip and was broken up after being towed to Belfast.

**Ethel May**

A regular Chester River trader between the wars. Roberts of Connah's Quay Post Office owned her in 1895. Richard Coppack one of her captains drowned from her in Mostyn Deeps. She was lost off the Pembroke coast in 1936.

**Excelsior**

Schooner of 90 tons completed in 1886 by Beshtons of Chester. She was bought by Coppacks in 1887 and sold to Ireland in 1911. She foundered off Ardmaine Head in 1917.

*Faithful*

Three-mast topsail schooner of 132 tons built by Ferguson & Gaird in 1887. She was stranded on Splaugh Rocks, County Wexford 1921.

*H.H.C.*

Hopper. This was the last ship to take a cargo, of brick, from Queensferry.

# Appendix III

## Other Wharves on the river Dee

The main ports and wharves from Chester to Point of Air have been listed with comments on each. But there were privately owned wharves, information about which are scant and in some cases unobtainable as it appears that records were either not kept, or destroyed. A third possibility of course is that they remain in private hands, having been handed down through the generations of the owning family. The following was obtained from *Maritime Wales 1906, Book 6*.

Chester Gas Works (2)    No record of any imports but a considerable amount of tar was exported from this wharf. It was a private wharf.

                                    Imports  –  unknown
                                    Exports  –  tar

Chester Corporation    They had their own wharf and the only mention of trade was of cement coming inwards.

Crane Wharf    Now the site of the Crosville Motor Services garage on Sealand Road. Trade was in timber, cement, machinery, flour, slate and grain.

Lamb's Wharf    Imports  –  slates and cement
                                    Exports  –  unknown

Dixon's Wharf    Imports  –  unknown
                                    Exports  –  unknown

Canal Wharf    Owned by the Shropshire Union Canal Company. Had a very small (unknown) annual cargo, mostly onto barges or from barges on the canal system.

Boat Builders Wharf    Unknown amount of trade in connection with the business.

| | |
|---|---|
| Cheese Storage Wharf | Situated in the bend of the Dee below Crane Wharf. Amount of trade not stated but mostly in connection with the cheese trade for which Cheshire was once a market leader. |
| Coed Talon Storage Wharf | Owned by the Dee Board and used to export artificial manure. Amounts unknown. |
| Queensferry (Joseph Turners Wharf) | Two stages here owned by the Gladstone family. Probably coal exports as the family had a lot of mining interests in the Ewloe & Hawarden areas. They were situated on the right-bank looking towards Chester from Queensferry bridge. |
| Dee Shipbuilders | Used in connection with their trade and the supply of motorised boats. |
| Queensferry (Coal Stages) | Used for the exporting of coal mostly to Ireland. The Aston Hall Coal Company had most of these small wharves. |
| Queensferry (Shipbuilders) | Situated downstream of the old ferry bridge, looking away from Chester towards the Ironworks. |
| Pentre | Probably in the area of the old Roman smelting-works at Fflint. It was stated in 1906 that there had been no traffic for many years. |
| Dee Bank Gutter | Somewhere near Bagillt and connected to the iron-ore trade, but no details of trade. |
| Williams & Robinsons Wharf | Imported a lot of iron to make anchors and other iron goods at their own factory, where |

heavy industry boilers were the speciality, and also shipping in later times.

At one time, no less than twenty-six wharves were in use on the short area of the Dee between Chester and Point of Air Colliery. This alone, without complete shipping records, shows how important and busy this area was, and how important the Dee was to north Wales and the part of England that was connected by the canal system.

# Appendix IV

## Angling, Wildlife and Conservation Groups on the river Dee

These are details of angling, wildlife and conservation groups that may be of interest, all of which welcome outside membership. Secretary/contact details were correct at the time of going to press.

**Bala and District Angling Association**
Fly-fishing only during the game season. Sunday fishing permitted and all ground baiting is prohibited except on Llyn Tegid (Bala Lake). The association offers salmon, sea trout, trout and excellent grayling fishing on the river Dee and surrounding streams.
Permits:  Siop yr Eryr, High Street, Bala. Tel: Bala 520370
          J A Jones, Post Office, Frongoch, Bala. Tel. Bala 520285

**Prince Albert Angling Society**
Fishing in various parts of north Wales.
Secretary: J A Turner, 15 Pexhill Drive, Macclesfield, Cheshire SK10 3LP. Tel: 01625 422010

**Corwen and District Angling**
Excellent fly-fishing for trout and grayling in Dee, Ceirw and Alwen and a small lake at Llandrillo. Salmon restricted to local persons residing within the catchment area for voting at Corwen. Persons residing outside Corwen are known as 'Country Members'.
Country Members Secretary: Mr Gordon Smith, Llais yr Afon, Bontuchel, Rhuthun LL15 2DE Tel. 01824 710609
Local Members Secretary: Mr Alan Roberts, 5 Bridge Street, Corwen. Tel. 01490 412925
*Fishing on this water is for members only. There are no day tickets.*

**Midland Fly-fishers**
Fly-fishing for trout and grayling on the Dee. Total of four miles of river on both banks.
Permits:
Season  Mr A R Collins, Pearl Assurance House, 4 Temple Row, Birmingham B2 5HG
Day     Mrs Jones-Roberts, Coed Iâl Farm, Glyndyfrdwy. Tel. 01490 430221

Berwyn Arms Hotel, Glyndyfrdwy. Tel. 01490 430210
Post Office, Glyndyfrdwy. Tel. 01490 430221

## Llangollen Angling Association

Mostly fly-fishing but some worm fishing allowed for trout and grayling
on the river Dee at Llangollen. Association controls over six miles of the
Dee. Day-tickets available for salmon fishing but above town bridge only.
Applications for full season salmon and trout tickets to the secretary. SAE
must be enclosed for all correspondence otherwise no replies.
Hon. Sec Mr W N Elbourn, 2 Green Lane, Llangollen, Clwyd.
Tickets: Hughes, Newsagents, Chapel Street, Llangollen. Tel. 01978
860155
    The society offers fishing with assistance for disabled anglers in the
summertime on the river. Full details from Hon. Sec.

## Maelor Angling

Restricted number of salmon members on this classic water. Applications
for trout and grayling season and day-tickets to Hon. Sec.
Mr K Bathers, Sunnyside, Hill Street, Cefn Mawr, Wrecsam. Tel: 01978
820608

## Bryn y Pys (Trout and Grayling)

There are two different fisheries of the same name here. The Bryn y Pys
Syndicate covers the salmon and sea trout fishing and the Bryn y Pys
Angling covers trout and coarse fishing. Excellent trout, grayling and
pike fishing on offer on the Dee, with an annual award for the best pike
and largest number of pike taken by rod and line.
Details: Mrs Ann Phillips, 2 Ruabon Road, Wrecsam,. Tel: 01978 351815

## Warrington Anglers

Have excellent facilities on the lower Dee at Worthenbury for salmon, sea
trout and coarse fishing both on Dee and feeder streams. Salmon fishing
is truly excellent in springtime and autumn with salmon straight in off
the tide. The first weir on the Dee is above this water.
Details: Hon. Sec. Mr Brown, 10 Dale Road, Golbourne, Warrington,
WA3 3PN. Tel. 01924 726917

    There are more than those listed above. Hotels and guesthouses also
sell day-tickets for some waters within the valley on production of a rod-
licence.
    Anyone requiring further details of the fishing on the Dee or its

carriers should contact: Environment Agency Wales (Asiantaeth yr Amgylchedd Cymru) on 01248 670770. Further information can be gleaned from their website:

www.asiantaeth-amgylchedd.cymru.gov.uk

## Nature Reserves

The principal body for nature conservation in north Wales is the North Wales Wildlife Trust, 376 High Street, Bangor, Gwynedd. They have over thirty nature reserves within north Wales and some are situated close to the Dee valley. Membership is open to everyone with branches and branch meetings at localities within the north Wales area. It publishes a bilingual quarterly colour magazine (Natur) on conservation and the work being done by the Trust, as well as contributions by members. Full details from the Bangor office. Tel: 01248 351541.
Further information can be found on the national website:

www.wildlifetrust.org.uk

## Deeside Naturalists' Society

This society has an excellent reserve situated on the former CEGB site at Connah's Quay power station on the main A548 coast road. There are four large wooden hides for viewing the estuary and its wildfowl, and several pools built by volunteers for the birds. The nature reserve is situated on the most important part of the Dee for waders, which can increase fivefold in wintertime. Peregrine falcons, buzzards, short-eared owls and many other raptors can also be seen on this reserve. Membership is open to everyone and details may be obtained from the secretary: Mrs Hazel Jones, 54 Upper Aston Hall Lane, Hawarden, Flintshire. Tel. 01244 533406

## Royal Society for the Protection of Birds

The RSPB owns vast amounts of land on both sides of the Dee estuary. Gayton Sands is on the English side while the Point of Air reserve is situated on the Welsh side. The telephone number of the RSPB warden responsible for the Dee estuary is 0151 336 7681. Further information can be gathered from the RSPB website, at:  www.rspb.org.uk

## Wirral Country Park

Situated on the English side of the estuary, this excellent park covers most of the English part of the estuary, foreshore and inland. The park has converted an old railway line into a country walk and conservation area and encourages public access, with massive improvements having been made to the foreshore area of the Dee. Whilst encouraging the public to use the facilities, it successfully balances nature conservation with these aims. Good access is provided for disabled persons. Full details from for the Wirral branch on Tel. 0151 648 4371 or from the Cheshire branch on 0151 327 5145. There is also a website at:

www.wirral.gov.uk/leisure/ranger

\*   \*   \*

All the listed organisations are powerful and influential in matters of conservation and welfare of wildlife. They enjoy considerable support from the public, councils and Members of Parliament as well as a good healthy membership from the general public.

Joining one of these groups gives you free and unlimited access to the reserves, and your subscription will go to assist the maintenance of the reserves. In doing so you will be assisting wildlife to survive in what is, for them, a cruel and unforgiving place thanks to the influence of man.